Human Resource Management in the Pornography Industry

David M. Kopp

Human Resource Management in the Pornography Industry

Business Practices in a Stigmatized Trade

palgrave
macmillan

David M. Kopp
Associate Vice Provost of Extended Learning
and Professor of Human Resource Development
Barry University
Miami Shores, FL, USA

ISBN 978-3-030-37658-1 ISBN 978-3-030-37659-8 (eBook)
https://doi.org/10.1007/978-3-030-37659-8

This Palgrave Macmillan imprint is published by the registered company Springer Nature Switzerland AG
The registered company address is: Gewerbestrasse 11, 6330 Cham, Switzerland

To Sandra, mi musa, mi amor. Te amo

Acknowledgments

My sincere gratitude for the many people who supported me while writing this book, especially my family.

Thanks to Palgrave-Macmillan, Marcus Ballenger, Kumaravel Senbagaraj, Susan Westendorf, Sophia Siegler, Siva Shukkanthy, the sponsoring editors and assistant editors; thanks also to Barry University.

The author would like to acknowledge the following people and organizations who contributed in some form to this book: Alix Lovell, Riley Reyes, Casey Calvert, Mark Spiegler, Alejandro Freixes, Antonia Crane, Jennifer Salgado, Dan Miller, XBIZ staff, AVN staff, APAC, APAG, Kenny B, Dave Fletcher, Carolina Potap, Katie Desiderio, Stephen Yagielowicz, Moe Helmy, and Ben Curtis.

Contents

Abbreviations

AA	Affirmative Action
AB	Assembly Bill
APAC	Adult Performers Advocacy Committee
APAG	Adult Performers Actors Guild
AVN	Adult Video News
B/G	Boy/Girl Scene
CSR	Corporate Social Responsibility
DYI	Do It Yourself (porn)
EEO	Equal Employment Opportunity
FSC	Free Speech Coalition
HRM	Human Resource Management
IEAU	International Entertainment Adult Union
IR	Interracial
KSA	Knowledge, Skills, and Attitudes
MILF	Mother I'd Like to Fuck
OSHA	Occupational Safety and Health Administration
ROI	Return on Investment
SHRM	Society of Human Resource Management
XBIZ	Portmanteau for X-rated Business

List of Figures

List of Tables

CHAPTER 1

Introduction: Counterintuitive Juxtapositions

Abstract In this introductory chapter, the author establishes the context by first providing an overview of the ubiquitous pornography industry, including a modern history, definitions (e.g., Supreme Court Justice Potter Stewart, "I know it when I see it."), as well as, describing the traditional business operation, which will introduce the reader to the human resource management (HRM) practices and how these traditional HR practices are utilized within this non-traditional industry. The chapter will also introduce the reader to the construct of so-called "dirty work" and the *organization-as-pariah*. This chapter will also give the reader an overview of the discipline of Human Resource Management.

Keywords Human Resource Management (HRM) · Pornography · Normative · Consent · Capitalism

D. M. Kopp, *Human Resource Management in the Pornography Industry*, https://doi.org/10.1007/978-3-030-37659-8_1

Evolution of a Book Idea

My interests gravitate toward how the typical existed against the background of the atypical. Whether learning that Hitler had one testicle (Fuchs, 1990),[1] Chairman Mao suffered from chronic constipation (Zhi-Sui, 2011), or Abraham Lincoln was a champion wrestler (Chapman, 2003), I always found myself just as captivated by the tangential endnotes and footnoted backstories within a book as much as the *raison d'être* of the book itself. In sum, I hold a fascination in how the ordinary is housed within extraordinary.[2]

During research for my second book, *Famous (and Infamous) Training: A Social History of Training and Development* (Kopp, 2018), I happened upon a new worker orientation video produced by the organization APAC. The 14-minute-plus video not only detailed what a newly hired worker could expect on the job, but also offered advice on such topics as job safety, performance improvement, and managing finances. As a human resources (HR) professional and academician, I thought it was a well-done, first-rate asynchronous job orientation video; however, what made it notable to me was not the information or advice given, but the context of this orientation video: APAC is the acronym for the Adult Performers Advocacy Council and their video is entitled, *Porn 101*.[3]

That the pornography industry had even produced a new worker orientation video is an example of the counterintuitive juxtapositions that this book takes on; that is, how human resource management (HRM) practices operationalize within the pornography industry.

Exploring HRM practices in situ within the pornography industry may be an especially constructive academic endeavor. In fact, the pornography industry faces much of the same operational considerations as traditional,

[1] Another example of this occurred when I was reading testimony from the Nuremberg trials (Office of Military Government for Germany [US], 1946). In the appendix was a "pullout" of the Nazi government; there was an organizational chart that had one of the job position boxes empty with no name, which left me with the dubious reflection that Hitler was hiring at the time.

[2] Many good books detail extraordinary aspects of the ordinary, from Jared Diamond's, Guns, Germs, and Steel, and Thomas Leddy's, The Aesthetics of Everyday Life, to David Bodanis', The Secret House, to name a few. Jason Grote and Joshua Glenn looked at the ordinary–extraordinary in their experiment, Significant Objects, of making significance out of ordinary things via narrative.

[3] https://www.youtube.com/watch?v=5hCTVWoLE0A.

for-profit industries. From increasing competition that threatens market share, new technology that impacts products and services, to health and workplace safety issues (Berg, 2015), the pornography industry, too, utilizes and applies many of the same human resource management (HRM) strategies that aim to recruit, select, and retain the best (sex) workers.

There is currently a dearth of research in the business studies literature vis-à-vis pornography (McKee, 2016; Rose, 2013). Voss (2012) pointed out that,

> ...much [of pornography research] focuses on individuals who are directly bodily involved in the production of sexually explicit material through their roles as actors and models rather than on those who are involved in the more business-related aspects including managers, accountants, and technicians. (p. 393)

And, while this book is not the first to explore the non-sex side of pornography (e.g., Berg, 2015; Bruckert & Parent, 2018; McKee, 2016; Tarrant, 2016[4])—many pornography company heads agree that they operate "like normal businesses" (Voss, 2012, p. 394)—it is sui generis in exploring how traditional human resource management systems are explicitly contextualized within the pornography industry.

Former porn actor and author Jiz Lee described how pornography research has "long trained its focus mostly on the sex side of the equation; however, like traditional workers, porn workers, too, share the goals of self-determination, autonomy, dignity, respect, and fair compensation" (Lee & Sullivan, 2016, p. 104)—an observation certainly worth acting upon. Additionally, from the perspective of human resource management itself, Klikauer (2014) puts forth that the moral philosophy of universalism dictates that the field of HRM considers human rights, especially as it relates to the most vulnerable and stigmatized in society—this presumably includes the sex workers in pornography, as well.

[4] Feminist researcher Heather Berg attended a panel of business owners and management trading tips and best practices at the 2011 Adult Entertainment Expo in Las Vegas; her conclusion was that porn's HR, specifically, "isn't a brave new world in personnel management at all, it is unexceptional to the core" (Berg, 2015, p. 1).

HRM—Overview and Placement Within

Nascent forms of human resource management (HRM) have existed throughout the history of collective living in civilization (Sims & Sauser, 2014; Tubey, Rotich, & Kurgat, 2015). During pre-historic times, for example, there were methods created for selection of tribal leaders, as well as the practice of safety and health while hunting was passed on from generation to generation (Tubey et al., 2015). The ancient Chinese dynasties used employee screening techniques, and in Babylonia training processes between artisan and apprentice were codified so that artisans could teach their crafts to the next generation so to ensure an adequate number of craftsmen (Kopp, 2014; Usher, 1920).

In the modern day, the field of HRM encompasses the oversight and administration of human capital within the organizational operation, including the functions of recruitment, staffing, compensation, workplace safety, workforce diversity and labor relations (Fig. 1.1). HRM is interdisciplinary, drawing up the social sciences of sociology, psychology, and economics.

In practice, HRM is carried out via the worldview of the practitioner; that is, philosophical perspectives to HRM vary within a *soft-hard* or transformational-transactional dichotomy (Bolton, 2010). Transformational HRM practice is patterned after the so-called Harvard Model (Beer, Spector, Lawrence, Mills, & Walton, 1984) where HRM is process-based, developmental and relationship-focused, what Management Professor Douglas McGregor called Theory Y (McGregor, 1960). Transactional HRM is modeled after the Michigan School (Fombrun, Tichy, & Devanna, 1984); here HRM is consequentialist, task-driven and focused on the economics and return on investment (ROI) of the human resources, endorsing McGregor's Theory X management assumption (McGregor, 1960).

The field and purpose of HRM is ever-changing as organizational landscapes change. Like a construct chameleon, HRM pivots as a function of the prevailing political ideology, new economic orders, and a more flexible capitalism (Bolton, 2010; Tubey et al., 2015). Yet, HRM paradigms notwithstanding, three overarching core principles of HRM (Armstrong, 1999) still consistently include:

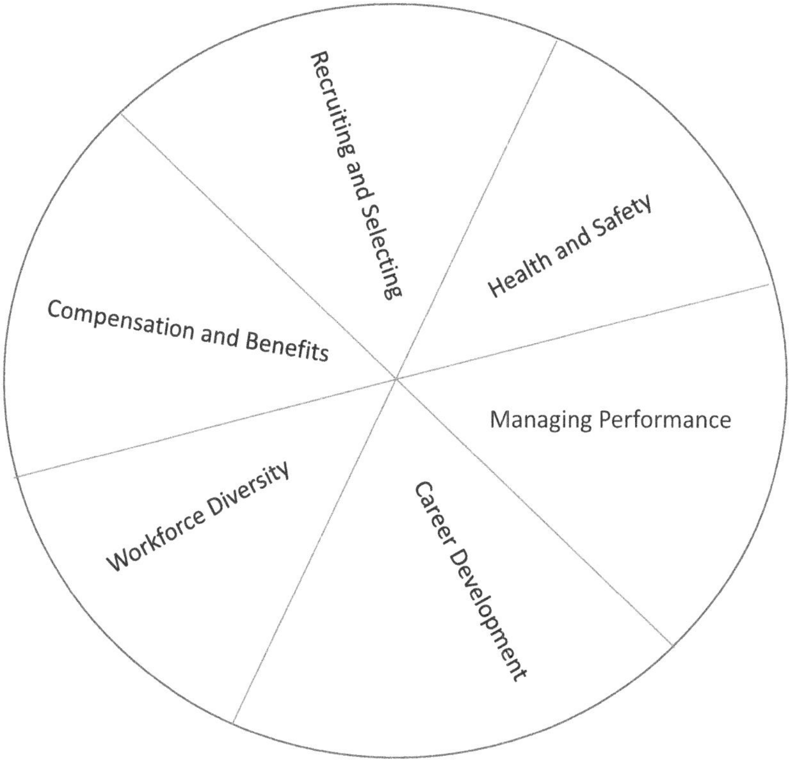

Fig. 1.1 The "slices" to the HRM pie (*Source* Author's rendition)

1. a recognition that human resources are the most important assets to an organization; businesses cannot be successful without effectively managing this resource.
2. that business success is most likely to be achieved if the policies and procedures for workers are closely linked with the achievement of business objectives.
3. that HRM's focus is to find, secure, and guide workers whose talents and desires are compatible with the operating needs and future goals of the company.

To be sure, HRM operationalizes itself within the pornography industry inimitably, especially given the precarity of the pornography industry (Berg & Penley, 2016). Yet, it is imperative to underscore that this book is not about pornography[5] per se; to that end, there will not be any Kantian debates on the morality of pornography,[6] protracted discussions on the patriarchal hegemony of porn (Tarrant, 2016), no narrative on the competing discourses of exploitation versus liberating sex work, nor even a proffered definition of pornography itself—here I invoke the assumption that, like American Supreme Court Justice Potter Stewart, the reader, too, knows it when he or she sees it.[7] As a practical matter, however, I do think that ethics professor David Rose is onto something when he puts forth a pornography-capitalism link; that is, ontologically speaking, sexually explicit material becomes pornography when it is produced for profit (Rose, 2013). Ultimately, it is APEG, the Adult Performers Actors Guild, a chapter under the *International Entertainment Adult Union*[8] and the only Department of Labor approved Parent Union representing the Adult Industry in the United States, who declares, "If there is no camera, you are not an adult performer."[9]

Additionally, this book is meant to be analytical and explorative, not prescriptive or programmatic, so while I comment on the existence of an HRM sub-system within the pornography industry, there is no plan to

[5] Even grammatically speaking and parsing out the book's main title: *Human Resource Management in the Pornography Industry*. Human Resource Management (HRM) *is* the subject while the pornography industry is the *object of the preposition*.

[6] Kant was critical of that which objectified women or challenged human autonomy.

[7] In 1964, the Supreme Court of the United States had to decide Jacobellis v. Ohio. Nico Jacobellis, the defendant in the case, was the manager of an art-house theater in Cleveland Heights, Ohio. Jacobellis was convicted of criminal charges and fined $2500 for the public exhibition of Louis Malle's film, *The Lovers* (*Les Amants*), at his theater. In deciding whether the film violated the First Amendment prohibition against obscene speech, Justice Potter Stewart famously said that, "I shall not today attempt further to define the kinds of material I understand to be embraced within that shorthand description; and perhaps I could never succeed in intelligibly doing so. But I know it when I see it, and the motion picture involved in this case is not that."

[8] The sex worker industry has had mixed results in their attempts to unionize, partly due to their independent contractor statuses. In 1996, the nude dancers at the Lusty Lady voted 57-15 to join a union, the first nude dancers to unionize in the nation: the Service Employees International Union, Local 790 (Gall, 2016) and personal interview with Antonia Crane, author and former adult dancer.

[9] http://entertainmentadultunion.com/index.cfm.

comment on the effectiveness or efficacy of said sub-system; the *quality* of the HRM systems is also not a focus in this book.

Reflections on This Project

While I felt confident that my three-plus decades of human resources (HR) experience uniquely qualified me to evaluate HRM practices in any industry, my aplomb was soon tempered by the cautionary tales articulated by other researchers (e.g., Ashforth & Kreiner, 1999; Lee, 1993; McKee, 2016) who had ventured into exploring the pornography industry academically.

There was no better account than that in Professor Georgina Voss's, *Treating it as a normal business: Researching the pornography industry* (2012). I immediately connected with Voss in that I, too, faced trivialization of my research.[10] Also, like Voss, I was subjected to constant questioning about the social and academic value of pornography from my peers, needing to regularly justify and validate the research. And, whereas Voss was asked by peers how she would be able to give academic presentations on the research "with a straight face" (p. 9); I was chronically asked how my wife felt about me interviewing "porn stars".[11]

These reactions were similar to those Bruckert and Parent (2018) received while researching for their book, *Getting Past 'the Pimp': Management in the Sex Industry*; they were summarily dismissed and criticized by some and said to be part of the "pimp lobby" for listening to what third parties (exploiters, pimps, and "traffickers") had to say.

Adding to the burden of pornography research is a presumption that academics not only bracket their biases (epoché), but their sexuality, too. To this point, renowned professor and researcher of sexualized media, Alan McKee noted that he could not recall an example of an academic employed at a university acknowledging in his or her research that they have a personal interest in pornography—the implication is that

[10] Several years ago, I had a similar "raised eyebrows" experience when NBA great Shaquille O'Neal enrolled into our doctoral program in Organizational Leadership. As his major professor, I ran across skepticism and disapproval from the subtle to overt within and without academia (see: https://www.youtube.com/watch?v=D13jdFtGh0Y).

[11] Voss draws upon researcher Raymond Lee's conclusions that where deviant groups are being studied research can become problematic for the researcher, in particular for researchers of human sexuality, who remark on their stigmatization by colleagues, university administrators and students (Lee, 1993).

consumers of pornography are still always *them*, and not us (McKee, 2016), thus touching upon a variant of Argyris' and Schon's (1996) premise of *espoused theory* versus *theory-in-use*, which further complicates this genre of research.

As I considered the epistemological strategies in exploring people qua sex workers in human resource management, I also contemplated pornography's placement within the sociocultural field and semiotics of organizational culture itself. Particularly, how the construct of pornography is linked to the terms, *norm, normal, or normative*. Applying these expressions to pornography became quite a thought experiment. As sociologists Wade, Hartmann, and Uggen (2016) define it, a 'norm' refers to that which is common or frequent, an evaluation of "what is." The term 'normal' is an assessment only as it relates to comparing it to something that is deemed *abnormal*. And, in contrast to both of these terms, 'normative' refers to a morally-endorsed ideal; it is prescriptive or "what ought to be."

So, for example, while some in the field of HR may consider watching pornography a norm, these same folks may not consider it normal. Further, some working in HR might claim watching pornography may be normal, but certainly not the norm. And, still another HR camp may claim watching pornography may be both normal and the norm, but not normative. A multi-permuted exercise, indeed!

Methodology

The resources I utilized included the extant peer-reviewed literature, especially in the present-day peer-reviewed journals, such as, *Porn Studies*. I also joined the email listserv of the APAG union's monthly newsletter, as well as utilized gray literature[12]; in addition, it was eighteen months of fieldwork that informed this book in no small part. I attended two adult conferences, AVN in Las Vegas and XBIZ in Miami. Each conference was three days in length, and it was in these conferences where I was able to

[12] Gray literature as in non-academic literature, including newspapers, magazines, and pamphlets.

become a participant researcher in the tradition of action research[13] using ethnographic observation.

While attending these conventions I had the opportunity to attend seminars, do in-depth semi-structured interviews with those in the industry both behind and in front of the camera, editors of trade publications, insurance brokers who serviced the pornography industry, talent agents, APAC officials, and owners of pornography companies. While my pool of interviewees was sufficient, many of those I interviewed asked not to be quoted directly or remain anonymous.

At XBIZ, I attended (YouTube™ Cam) workshops, and seminars that discussed the state of the industry, including legal challenges. For example, and to be discussed, during this time the pornography industry was unified in demanding the social platform Instagram cease in censoring adult performers accounts; in fact, many accounts were deleted due to nudity policies.[14]

Limitations and Delimitations

Importantly, this book is not intended to be an unabridged analysis on human resource practices within the pornography industry—indeed, my intent is solely to introduce readers to (and raise awareness of) these strange bedfellows. By no means, do I proclaim that my evaluation and fieldwork should be generalized—in the absence of a controlled setting it would be difficult—my only goals are to share my experiences in the field, stimulate interesting policy questions for stakeholders, and to what future researchers' appetite with this primer.

Furthermore, this qualitative evaluation of HRM in the pornography industry was carried out within certain boundaries and demarcations. For example, by intention, I rejected exploring forms of pornography that would fall under coercive, exploitive, and, otherwise, harmful context and

[13] Action research seeks transformative change through the simultaneous process of taking action and doing research, which are linked together by critical reflection. Kurt Lewin first coined the term "action research" in 1944. In his 1946 paper *Action Research and Minority Problems* Lewin described action research as a comparative research on the conditions and effects of various forms of social action and research leading to social action that uses "a spiral of steps, each of which is composed of a circle of planning, action and fact-finding about the result of the action" (Argyris, Putnam, & Smith, 1985).

[14] https://www.xbiz.com/news/243584/instagram-and-the-war-on-porn-an-xbiz-explainer.

behaviors. Much of the basis for this exclusion followed Wertheimer's (2003) *Principles of Valid Consent (PVC)* framework where the ontology of sexual consent is discussed not only from a legal and moral standpoint, but particularly from the construct of autonomy, thus excluding that which would involve sex trafficking explicitly.

In particular, I proceeded with an assessment of HRM in pornography within the domain of sex work as contrasted by sex trafficking.[15] Sex work is defined as when a person willingly takes part in consensual sex and the individual's human rights are not violated (George, Vindhya, & Ray, 2010); that is, those conditions are jointly necessary and sufficient. This is set apart from sex trafficking, when an individual takes part in sexual activity through threat, abduction, or other means of coercion, perceived, or real.[16]

Additionally, utilizing the Palermo Protocols,[17] this evaluation excludes those genres of pornography that are considered illegal such as child pornography, bestiality, incest, and the relatively new category of *revenge porn*.

Because most who work in pornography are independent contractors[18] and not employees of an organization, many aspects of human resource management practice will not be applicable or observable; in fact, since most sex workers are independent contractors, they, in effect, become their own HR departments. It is also worth noting that, while sex work does have some universalities associated with it, my evaluation of HRM practices in the pornography industry was limited to the United States

[15] I acknowledge that some sex work scholars still critique this dichotomy, noting that the construct of consent operates on an ambiguous continuum.

[16] https://www.stopthetraffik.org/sex-trafficking-vs-sex-work-understanding-difference/.

[17] The Palermo Protocols were adopted by the United Nations to supplement the 2000 Convention against Transnational Organized Crime (the Palermo Convention). They include the protocol to Prevent, Suppress, and Punish Trafficking in Persons, especially Women and Children.

[18] It is worth noting that the pornography industry is not unique in subcontracting out their workers. In today's practice of HRM, there are growing models that move away from the traditional employer–employee relationship. For example, Employee Leasing, where employees are leased and the company pays a fee to the leasing firm or the consultancy that handles employee benefits, payroll, and all other HR functions on behalf of the client company. Outsourcing, too, where companies outsource or assign the task of recruitment to the third-party specialist, who then carry out all the recruitment activities which would have been done in-house otherwise (Werner & DeSimone, 2011, p. 283).

only. And, while I endeavored to interview both male and female adult performers, the vast majority of my fieldwork's convenience sample was female performers (most of the non-performer interviews were male).

Finally, to be sure, *this is not your father's pornography*[19]; that is to say, this would have been quite another book had it been written even a decade ago. The pornography industry today is a very different industry than it was, not only due to internet porn, but specifically to "DYI" online, unregulated amateur porn. Nowadays, much of porn is viewed on easily accessible "tube sites," such as YouPorn™ and Pornhub™; as a result, this has impacting the established pornography industry—in fact, applications for porn-shoot permits reportedly fell by ninety-five percent between 2012 and 2015 (Forrester, 2016).

Thus, while there are clearly distinctions to be made, as will be described, HRM processes are nevertheless conspicuous in the business of pornography, and what follows is my review of *Human Resource Management in the Pornography Industry: Business Practices in a Stigmatized Trade.*

References

Argyris, C., Putnam, R., & Smith, D. (1985). *Action science: Concepts, methods and skills for research and intervention.* San Francisco: Jossey-Bass.

Argyris, C., & Schon, D. (1996). *Organizational learning II*: Reading, MA. Addison-Wesley.

Armstrong, M. (1999). *A handbook of human resource management practice.* London, UK: Kogan Page Ltd.

Ashforth, B., & Kreiner, G. (1999). How can you do it?: Dirty work and the challenge of constructing a positive identity. *The Academy of Management Review, 24*(3), 413–434.

Beer, M., Spector, B. A., Lawrence, P. R., Mills, D. Q., & Walton, R. E. (1984). *Managing human assets.* New York: Free Press.

Berg, H. (2015). Business a usual. *Jacobinmag.*

Berg, H., & Penley, C. (2016). Creative precarity in the adult film industry. In M. Curtin & K. Sanson (Eds.), *Precarious Creativity* (pp. 159–171). Oakland: University of California Press.

[19]The term "Golden Age of Porn" refers to a 15-year period (1969–1984) in American pornography in which sexually explicit films experienced positive attention from mainstream cinemas, movie critics, and the general public (Gall, 2016).

Bruckert, C., & Parent, C. (2018). *Getting past 'the pimp': Management in the sex industry*. Toronto: University of Toronto Press.
Bolton, S. (2010). *Critical human resource management*. New York, NY: Sage.
Chapman, M. (2003). *The sport of Lincoln*. United States: Culture House Books.
Fombrun, C., Tichy, N., & Devanna, M. (1984). *Strategic human resource management*. New York, NY: Wiley.
Forrester, K. (2016). Making sense of modern pornography. *The New Yorker*.
Fuchs, T. (1990). *The Hitler fact book*. United States: Fountain Books.
Gall, G. (2016). *Sex worker unionization: Global developments, Challenges and Possibilities*. London, UK: Palgrave Macmillan.
George, A., Vindhya, U., & Ray, S. (2010). Sex trafficking and sex work: Definitions, debates and dynamics—A review of literature. *Economic and Political Weekly, 45*(17), 64–73. Retrieved from www.jstor.org/stable/25664387.
Klikauer, T. (2014). *Seven moralities of human resource management*. United Kingdom: Palgrave Macmillan.
Kopp, D. M. (2014). *Human resource development: Performance through learning*. San Diego: Bridgepoint Education.
Kopp, D. M. (2018). *Famous (and Infamous) workplace and community training: A social history of training and development*. United States: Palgrave Macmillan.
Lee, R.M. (1993). *Doing research on sensitive topics*. London: Sage.
Lee, J., & Sullivan, R. (2016). Porn and labour: The labour of porn studies. *Porn Studies*, *3*(2), 104–106. London: Taylor & Francis.
McGregor, D. (1960). *The human side of enterprise*. New York: McGraw-Hill.
McKee, A. (2016). Pornography as a creative industry: Challenging the exceptionalist approach to pornography. *Porn Studies,* 3, 107–119. https://doi.org/10.1080/23268743.2015.1065202.
Office of Military Government for Germany (US). (1946). *Nurnberg military tribunals: Indictments, case no. 1–12*. Nurnberg: OMGG.
Rose, D. (2013). *The ethics and politics of pornography*. United Kingdom: Palgrave Macmillan.
Sims, R. R., & Sauser, W. I. (2014). *Legal and regulatory issues in human resources management*. Charlotte, NC: Information Age Publishing, Incorporated.
Tarrant, S. (2016). *The pornography industry: What everyone needs to know*. New York, NY: Oxford University Press.
Tubey, R., Rotich, J., & Kurgat, A. (2015). History, evolution and development of human resource management: A contemporary perspective *European. Journal of Business and Management*, *7*(9), 139–148.
Usher, A. P. (1920). *An introduction to the industrial history of England*. New York: Houghton Mifflin.

Voss, G. (2012). Treating it as a normal business: Researching the pornography industry. *Sexualities,* 15, 391–410. https://doi.org/10.1177/1363460712439650.

Wade, L., Hartmann, D., & Uggen, C. (2016). *Assigned: Life with gender*. New York, NY: W. W. Norton.

Werner, J. M., & DeSimone, R. L. (2011). *Human resource development*. Mason, OH: Cengage Learning.

Wertheimer, A. (2003). *Consent to sexual relations*. Cambridge, UK: Cambridge University Press.

Zhi-Sui, L. (2011). *The private life of chairman Mao*. New York: Random House Publishing Group.

CHAPTER 2

Recruiting, Selecting, and Retaining Talent

Abstract In this chapter, the author describes the processes of how workers in pornography are recruited and/or endeavor to work in the porn industry. As the author has seen, like in traditional organizations, employers in pornography are looking for workers who are motivated, have a great attitude and good work ethic. For example, before they cast someone, producers of pornography want to tell a little bit about a prospect's psychological state, too. How eager they are to do it? How motivated by money they are to do it, as opposed to the fun aspect? Specific worker profiles will be explored, as well as, worker turnover and retention.

Keywords Dirty work · Taint · Stigma · Onboarding · Job analysis · Labor pool

The staffing function is a fundamental component of human resource management (HRM), and undergirding the purposeful HRM staffing operation are the recruitment, selection, and retention sub-systems. An antecedent condition to both recruitment and selection are job market conditions and in the pornography industry it is a buyer's market; that is, like the unicorn and astatine, rare is the porn production that is halted due to a shortage of eligible workers.

D. M. Kopp, *Human Resource Management in the Pornography Industry*, https://doi.org/10.1007/978-3-030-37659-8_2

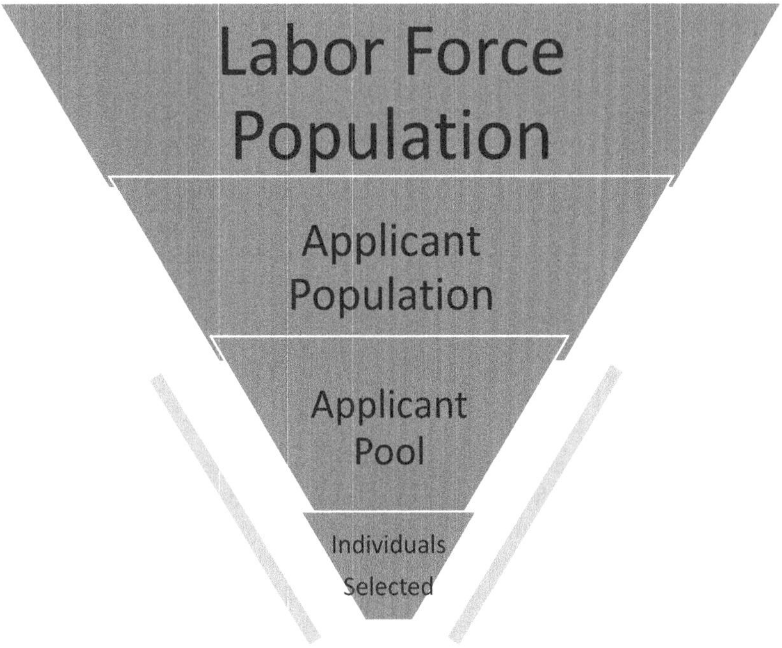

Fig. 2.1 Typical staffing funnel (*Source* Author's rendition)

In fact, unlike the conventional staffing funnel whereby the number of workers selected for a job is traditionally a smaller subset of the eligible pool who applied (Fig. 2.1), in porn, interviews from my field research lay bare the idea that pornography's applicant pool is virtually the same as the individuals selected (Fig. 2.2).

Not surprisingly, the pornography industry's eager labor pool is a direct function of the most potent factor as to why one goes into the adult entertainment industry in the first place: *the money*. In their 2012 study, Griffith, Adams, Hart, and Mitchell (2012) asked 176 porn actresses to describe the reasons that drove them to their profession and more than half responded money while a distant second was the actual sex.

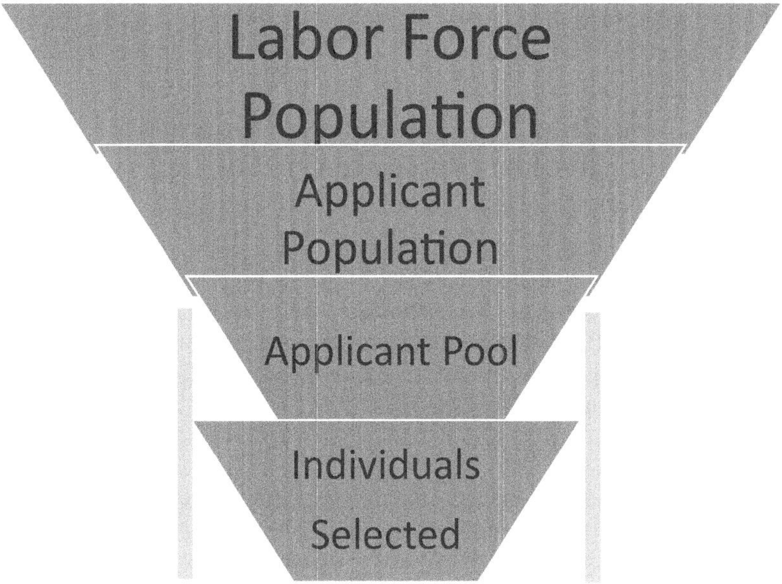

Fig. 2.2 Pornography industry's staffing funnel (*Source* Author's rendition)

Help Wanted: A Sex Worker by Any Other Name

Workers seeking employment—or more accurately, self-employment—in the pornography industry are thought to be part of the stratification of sex workers. Exner, Wylie, Leura, and Parrill (1977) were the first to classify types of sex workers by differentiating them into intra-occupational categories based on their mode of operation. For example, class 1 sex workers were considered "high status call girls," class III were "streetwalkers" and class V were "drugs-for-sex streetwalkers."

According to Nadal (2017), the literature on sex work began to expand in the 1990s and 2010s to broaden the classification of sex work not only by physical location, but also to include the work environment itself. That is, a differentiation was made between outdoor sex work (e.g., street-walking prostitutes) from those sex workers who worked in indoor, closed environments (e.g., peep-shows or within brothels).

Today's sex work categories are further distinguished between live, face-to-face sex work and two-dimensional synchronous sex work as seen with live webcams and sex workers who model and act asynchronously via DVD movies and through the Internet, viz., the pornography industry.

Jobs in Porn—Stigma, Dirty Work, and Taint, Oh My...

In addition to pornography being treated as "qualitatively different from other forms of work" (McKee, 2016, p. 3), jobs in pornography are stigmatized and are labeled as a class of "dirty work" (Attwood, 2009). Dirty work was a construct first introduced by sociologist Everett Hughes (Hughes, 1951, 1958, 1962); Hughes furthered his notion of dirty work recalling the context of a notable example being the German Nazi's final solution to the "problem" of the Jews.

Hughes wrote that:

> ...every occupation is not one, but several activities; some of them are the *dirty work* [italics added] of that trade. It may be dirty in one of several ways. It may be simply physically disgusting. It may be a symbol of degradation, something that wounds one's dignity. Finally, it may be dirty work in that it in some way goes counter to the more heroic of our moral conceptions. (1951, p. 62)

The concept of dirty work is typically thought of as a subset of the larger notion of *stigma* (Rogelberg, 2006). Goffman (1963/1990) defined stigma as an attribute, behavior, or reputation which is socially discrediting in a particular way; he described it as causing an individual to be mentally classified by others as undesirable and, specifically, included occupations or tasks that are perceived to be degrading on a physical, social, or moral level; Ashforth and Kreiner (1999) went on to describe these as levels or dimensions of *taint*.[1]

According to Grandy (2008),

> as a form of dirty work, exotic dancing, for example, can be seen to be physically tainted (e.g., in contact with bodily fluids through unprotected client/customer interactions or dancers using the same stage and poles to do tricks without cleaning between sets), socially tainted (e.g., associated with "sleazy" men, working in dangerous parts of the city) or morally

[1] Rivera (2015) also included a fourth level of as emotionally *tainted*.

tainted (e.g., commercialization of sex, public sex, sex outside of marriage). (p. 177)

The range of jobs considered stigmatized or dirty work is diverse (e.g., bill collectors, dentists, funeral directors, managerial work, taxi drivers) and includes sex workers (Blithe & Wolfe, 2019). In Ashforth's and Kreiner's matrix, pornography is stratified as a "low prestige, morally tainted" job (Table 2.1).

That the pornography industry is marginalized for its so-called dirty work enables this book to be a form of *emancipatory research* (Barton, 2005), whereby the inquiry is designed with and for subjects who may be marginalized for reasons of race, gender, sexual orientation, disability, economic background., and—relevant here—stigmatized jobs. And, there may be value in this because, as Voss (2012, 2015) pointed out, due to the stigma and dirty work classification, legitimate organizational systems and processes within what Schussler (2013) called the "pornographic apparatus" have been given less consideration and critical examination, and are notably absent in business studies.

Table 2.1 Dimensions of job taint

	Relative prestige	
Primary taint	*Low*	*High*
Physical	• Animal control officers; animal caretakers, except farm) • Exterminators; pest control occupations) Roofers	• Emergency room nurses • Firefighters • Morticians
Social	• Chauffeurs; taxicab drivers • Correctional officers • Welfare aides	• Internal affairs police officers; detectives • Social services counselors • Surveillance/probation officers
Moral	• Collection agents • Exotic entertainers; artists, performers, and related workers • Used car salespeople; sales workers, motor vehicles and boats	• Abortion clinic medial staff • Animal researchers; biological and life scientists) • Personal injury lawyers

Source Adapted from Ashforth and Kriener (1999)

Pornography's Recruiting and Staffing—It Takes an X-Rated Village

How a would-be adult performer is recruited for and gets his or her first gig is relatively straightforward. Most adult productions are cast by the producer or director by looking at various agency websites or communicating with agents via email or word of mouth. Some amateur, lower profile sites may utilize resources such as SexyJobs.com, adult-staffing.com, and Craigslist, where a prospective adult performer can upload her resume,[2] and various other online ads to recruit potential models.

XBIZ's Managing Editor Alejandro Freixes—who I was introduced to at XBIZ 2019—interviewed Vanessa Eve the Director of Talent Recruiting for Streamate, a webcam porn site, which was an enlightening look on a marketing strategy for attracting potential talent to join an adult platform:

> My approach for attracting new talent to Streamate has certainly evolved, especially as live cams continued to boom over the past handful of years. When I began recruiting for Streamate, I marketed for talent using more traditional avenues, running print ads in alternative weeklies and college newspapers, and posting banner and classified ads on adult job sites. I took unconventional routes at times, like responding to local escort ads. On a couple of occasions, I was kicked out of gentlemen's clubs because they suspected I was an escort trying to poach patrons, when I was really there to talk to dancers and just maybe slip in a few business cards. (Freixes, 2017)

For a small number of high-profile movies each year, there may be a casting call. Estimates given were approximately five casting calls per year at most; seasoned producers get to know a big percentage of the pool of adult performers and cast entire movies in many cases based on relationships. Even when a producer was friends with the model, they still went through that performer's agent to book. Social media now plays a significant role in the casting process, too. Some producer/directors will put out the word on their Twitter account that they are looking for a

[2] Note: Many of the skills listed above (e.g., self-starter, works well under pressure, and skilled multi-tasked transcends industries. Any organization's HR department would seek out such an applicant.

certain type of model to fill a role for their movie. Not only does this generates instant engagement from their followers, but it is also a form of crowd-sourcing to fill roles.

McKee (2016) recounts in Waskul (2004) how Taylor Marsh, who worked as the managing editor of the pornographic website Danni's Hard Drive, explained how, in recruiting staff into the company she would look specifically for people who had transferable talents from other sectors of the Creative Industries:

> The first line on his resume stated that he'd managed the talent for Barnum and Bailey Circus. That was all I needed to know. Anyone who could manage circus talent definitely had the qualifications to coordinate the crew I needed managed, the strippers, models, and XXX-rated porn actresses of the adult entertainment industry. (Marsh, 2000, 2004, p. 250)[3]

Pornography's On-Boarding Culture

What I learned from my field interviews that the on-boarding process for *new-to-the-business* performers was not markedly different than traditional job orientations. Several interviewees described how they were professionally greeted and introduced upon walking onto a set for the first time. Many were offered snacks, water, and shown the restrooms. For productions that had the budgets, there were make-up artists; otherwise, the female performer would have been asked to come make-up ready.

Much like in the traditional new employee form-heavy HRM world,[4] during the orientation, the performer is given paperwork to complete; the paperwork includes record-keeping documentation such as identification papers including the "2257 form" (Fig. 2.3) that officially ensures that adult performers participating in the production of the film are verified to

[3] Interestingly, and only slightly off topic, HRM practices were evaluated for Cirque du Soleil, the Canada based circus entertainment company. The study highlights the recruitment and selection, training, performance appraisal, culture, and work environment at Cirque. It also examines how Cirque managed cultural diversity of its workforce (Gupta & Pawar, 2007).

[4] The range of HR forms usually covers much more due to the aspects of managing an "employer/employee relationship" vs. independent contractors. Traditional HRM forms include: Candidate Evaluation Forms, Employment Applications, New Employee/Onboarding, Performance Review Forms, Termination Forms, Form W-4, I9 form and related notices.

TITLE or SHOOT ID of the work in which Model appears: ______________________

Model ID: ______

MODEL RELEASE, CONSENT AND WAIVER AGREEMENT RECORDS KEEPING COMPLIANCE FORM
PURSUANT TO 18 U.S.C. § 2257 & 28 CFR §75.1 et seq.

THIS IS A LEGALLY BINDING CONTRACT. READ IT CAREFULLY

1. SERVICES.
On behalf of ________ (hereafter 'Producer'), the undersigned, (hereafter 'Model'), will render services as an actor/model on the date given below.

Model Legal Name: __________________________________ Maiden Name:
(Full Current Legal Name: First, Middle, Last)
All Names:
____
(List all names you have used in the past, including Stage Names, Aliases, Professional Names etc.)
Stage name for this production: ___________________________
Date of Birth: ________________ Phone: _____________

Email Address: _____________

(Month, Day and Year)

Government Issued Picture Identification
Type: ______________________
ID #: _______________________
___ Please check this box if you have moved since you last shot with us
___ Please check this box if you want us to make your check out to your corporation

Name of corporation: ____________________

Model, _____________________________________, solemnly declares under penalty of perjury that (PLEASE INITIAL):
(legal name)
I have read and thoroughly understand the terms and conditions of the Services I will offer.
I understand that behind-the-scenes footage may be shot throughout the production date, the same grant of rights applies to this material.
_____
I do not have any health condition or sexually transmitted diseases that would expose others to negative health conditions from engaging in sexual activities with me. Producer requires safe sex practices.

Fig. 2.3 Form 2257 verifying identification that adult performers are 18 or older (*Source* KINK.com)

be above the age of 18.[5] Also, as self-employed workers, adult performers usually complete the IRS W9 form, as well.

Prior to the shoot the producer, director, and other talent may ask to see proof of the latest STI-free blood tests results—this can take on the form of showing others (from your phone) that you are logged onto to the Performer Availability Screening Services (PASS) database and then display your results. As discussed further in Chapter 7, Health and Safety, the standard protocol for adult talent involves voluntary testing done every fourteen days. As described by Tarrant (2016),

> [T]hese tests are conducted at a variety of private testing sites, the bulk of which are in Los Angeles County, with an additional location in Las Vegas and another in Miami. Once tests are completed, the results are entered into the (PASS), a database that is maintained by the Free Speech Coalition (FSC). (p. 128)

While recruiting and selection channels in the pornography industry are robust and uncomplicated, retention of sex workers is tenuous, at best. Adult performers in pornography are peripatetic and itinerant by nature with the average tenure for a worker in the industry being less than a year according to adult performer agent Marc Spiegler (Speigler, personal communication, February, 2019).

And, whereas the porn industry utilizes the traditional job analysis and notion of Person-Job fit (Fleishman, 1992; Harrow, 1972) quite literally, this underscores the fact that the same unassuming processes for staffing sit atop complex workplace constructs that affect tenure and job well-being, irrespective of a stigmatized trade (to be discussed in Chapter 3).

[5] The Child Protection and Obscenity Enforcement Act of 1988, title VII places stringent record-keeping requirements on the producers of actual, sexually explicit materials. The guidelines for enforcing these laws (colloquially known as 2257 regulations) are part of the United States Code of Federal Regulations that, require producers of sexually explicit material to obtain proof of age for every model they shoot and retain those records. Federal inspectors may at any time launch inspections of these records and prosecute any infraction (Source: http://www.zei2257.com/FR-28CFR75-20081218.html). Similarly, there is the CAN-SPAM Act (Controlling the Assault of Non-Solicited Pornography and Marketing Act), congressional legislation that regulates commercial emails (e.g., solicited to participate or promotion) and sets clearly defined opt-out standards.

References

Ashforth, B., & Kreiner, G. (1999). How can you do it?: Dirty work and the challenge of constructing a positive identity. *The Academy of Management Review, 24*(3), 413–434.

Attwood, F. (Ed.) (2009). *Dirty work: researching women and sexual representation.* London: Taylor & Francis.

Barton, L. (2005). Emancipatory research and disabled people: Some observations and questions. *Educational Review, 57*(3), 317–327.

Blithe, S. J., Mohr, B., & Wolfe, A. W. (2019). *Sex and stigma: Stories of everyday life in Nevada's legal brothels.* United States: New York University Press.

Exner, J. E., Wylie, J., Leura, A., & Parrill, T. (1977). Some psychological characteristics of prostitutes. *Journal of Personality Assessment, 41*(5), 474–485. https://doi.org/10.1207/s15327752jpa4105_3.

Fleishman, E. A. (1992). *Psychomotor, physical, and interpersonal requirements of work: Implications for revision of the dictionary of occupational titles (DOT).* Salt Lake City, UT: Department of Employment Security.

Freixes, A. (2017, September 14). Vanessa Eve Orchestrates Stellar Talent Recruitment. *XBIZ.*

Goffman, E. (1963/1990). *Stigma: Notes on the management of spoiled identity.* Harmondsworth: Penguin.

Grandy, G. (2008). Managing spoiled identities: Dirty workers' struggles for a favourable sense of self. *Qualitative Research in Organizations and Management, 3*(3), 176–198.

Griffith, J., Adams, L., Hart, C., & Mitchell, S. (2012). Why become a pornography actress? *International Journal of Sexual Health, 24,* 165–180.

Gupta, V., & Pawar, M. (2007). *Cirque du Soleil's human resource management practices* (p. 16). Babson College: IBS Center for Management Research.

Harrow, A. (1972). *Taxonomy of psychomotor domain: A guide for developing behavioral objectives.* New York: David McKay.

Hughes, E. C. (1951). Studying the nurse's work. *American Journal of Nursing, 51*(May), 294–295.

Hughes, E. C. (1958). *Men and their work.* Glencoe, IL: Free Press.

Hughes, E. C. (1962). Good people and dirty work. *Social Problems, 10*(1), 3–11. https://doi.org/10.2307/799402.

Marsh, T. (2000). *My year in smut: The internet escapades inside Danni's hard drive.* Bloomington, IN: AuthorHouse.

Marsh, T. (2004). My year in smut: Inside Danni's hard drive. In D. D. Waskul (Ed.), *Net.sexxx: Readings in sex, pornography and the internet* (pp. 237–258). New York: Peter Lang.

McKee, A. (2016). Pornography as a creative industry: Challenging the exceptionalist approach to pornography. *Porn Studies, 3*(2), 107–119. https://doi.org/10.1080/23268743.2015.1065202.

Nadal, K. L. (2017). *The SAGE encyclopedia of psychology and gender*. Los Angeles, CA: Sage.

Rivera, K. D. (2015). Emotional taint: Making sense of emotional dirty work at the U.S. border patrol. *Management Communication Quarterly, 29*(2), 198–228. https://doi.org/10.1177/0893318914554090.

Rogelberg, S. G. (2006). *Encyclopedia of industrial and organizational psychology*. Thousand Oaks, CA: Sage.

Schussler, A. (2013). Pornography and postmodernism. *Postmodern Openings, 4*(3), 7–23.

Speigler, M. (2019, February 2019). [Personal Communication].

Tarrant, S. (2016). *The pornography industry: What everyone needs to know*. New York, NY: Oxford University Press.

Voss, G. (2012). Treating it as a normal business: Researching the pornography industry. *Sexualities, 15*(3/4), 391–410. https://doi.org/10.1177/1363460712439650.

Voss, G. (2015). *Stigma and the shaping of the pornography industry*. Oxford: Taylor & Francis.

Waskul, D. D. (2004). *Net.seXXX: Readings on sex, pornography, and the internet*. New York: Peter Lang.

CHAPTER 3

Managing Performance

Abstract In this chapter, the author explores performance management and the skill sets needed to perform in adult films. Male performers, for example, have their own unique set of challenges. According to adult film producer and director, Dan Leal, "Every man is on penis pill supplements or injects...any guy who says he isn't is lying. In the real world, you don't have sex for this long; that's the reality." While performing, actors must focus on such things as timing, where the camera is, and what angle might be best for the camera. The author will seek out additional interviews using narrative inquiry to glean a day in the life of an adult performer and the knowledge, skills, and attitudes required to do the job.

Keywords Gig worker · Performance evaluation · Job aids · Ontology · Performance management · Psychomotor

Performance management—what workers do, how they do it, and what results are achieved—is a principal part of the Human Resource Management (HRM) system. Because the construct of performance is "largely a *practice-based* phenomenon there has been a dearth of philosophical consideration" (Swanson & Holton, 2009, p. 132). And, while it is true

D. M. Kopp, *Human Resource Management in the Pornography Industry*, https://doi.org/10.1007/978-3-030-37659-8_3

that the on-the-job, camera-facing[1] work enacted in pornography is not particularly nuanced—performing a sex act on camera being primarily a *psychomotor* event ala Fleishman's taxonomy (Fleishman, 1954)[2]—pornography's gig[3] work is, nevertheless, undergirded by the concepts, theories, and paradigms of job performance. This includes the principles of work psychology, viz., self-determination (Gagné & Deci, 2005), self-efficacy (Bandura, 1977), work identity (Gini, 1998), job engagement (Amabile & Kramer, 2013), and the meaning of work itself (Anderson, Ones, Sinangil, & Viswesvaran, 2001; Bali, 2015; Lee & Sullivan, 2016; Rousseau, 1989). Such constructs moderate the work experience, serving as performance drivers not only for the traditional employee, but also the sex worker, as well. This confirms the centrality of work in one's life, regardless of heavy lifting or heavy thinking.

The Ontology of Workplace Performance

As with all jobs, performance on the job is a function of—and evaluated on—the nature of the job itself. Within the HRM literature there are numerous perspectives of workplace performance (e.g., Alagaraja, 2012; Armstrong & Appelbaum, 2003; Kopp, 2014; Rousseau, 1989; Rummler & Brache, 1995; Swanson, 1995; Swanson & Holton, 2009; Weiss, 2013; Williams, 1998).

Swanson and Holton (2009) outlined three philosophical paradigms for job performance that tethered well to the themes emerged during my field research in the pornography industry, namely:

[1] It should be noted that in the sex industry most workers are "non-sexual"; that is, drivers, accountants...and magazine editors (Agustin, 2005, p. 618).

[2] Fleishman's Taxonomy of Motor Abilities include physical proficiency abilities of strength, flexibility, balance, coordination, and endurance.

[3] Gig work is part of the gig economy, defined as an environment in which temporary positions or contingent work is common and organizations contract independent workers for short-term engagements. These contingent workers or "giggers" are also known as freelancers, independent professionals, temporary contract workers, independent contractors, or consultants (Kessler, 2019), thus including workers in the pornography industry, as well. The growing need for agility in how companies do business means an 'on demand' workforce allows organizations to staff up and down as required. It is predicted that by 2020 gig workers will comprise up to 30% of an organization's workforce.

- performance as necessary for economic activity
- performance as a natural outcome of human activity; and
- performance as a tool for organizational oppression.

Performance as Necessary for Economic Activity

Not surprisingly, within the pornography industry, monetary themes and motivations are expressed the most frequently (compensation in the pornography industry will be discussed in a subsequent chapter); in this perspective, performance is considered value neutral and utilitarian; that is, this view sees performance as neither inherently good nor bad, but rather as a means to economic ends.

My interviews with adult performers underscored this theme, particularly; each stressed how—especially in the face of their accrued "college debt"—pornography offered a way to counter the financial obligations and responsibilities.[4] Tarrant (2016) described how adult performer, Belle Knox, a first-year Duke University student who was outed as a porn performer candidly responded to the media firestorm by explaining the "high cost of college and how doing porn helped her pay for tuition" (p. 62). In fact, Griffith, Adams, Hart, and Mitchell (2012) found that 53% of those in adult entertainment went into the industry because of the money and 41% of respondents stated that money was what they liked the most about industry. Many adult performers believe that pornography is an easy way to make a substantial amount of money in a short amount of time.

This pragmatic perspective of performance with its rational exchange sees performance as necessary for individuals to not only earn livelihoods, but sometimes for subsistence, as well, which Tarrant (2016) called *survival sex work* that is performed for immediate, primary needs such as food, clothing, and shelter.

[4] A recent study found that involved interviews with 300 exotic dancers found there that a quarter had advanced degrees, while one in three women were in some form of education, with about 14% working to fund an undergraduate course and about 6% to fund a postgraduate degree (https://www.reuters.com/article/us-britain-lapdancing/study-finds-quarter-of-uk-lap-dancers-have-degrees-idUSTRE67Q2YW20100827).

Performance as a Natural Outcome of Human Activity

In this view—which is also consistent with Maslow's (1943) proposition that human beings pursue self-actualization—work (and working) is accepted as a natural part of human existence and regarded as a basic human need. Industrial psychologist Howard Weiss (2013) put forth that *working* is part of human nature. In this perspective of performance, the premise is that "few people are content *not* [italics added] to perform" (Swanson & Holton, 2009, p. 261).

McKee (2016) pointed out that the pornography industry, too—though frequently set apart from other forms of culture—is itself a creative industry and part of the aesthetic system of entertainment (both high- and lowbrow); these industries have at their origin individual creativity and skill sets. In her research of women in pornography, associate professor of feminist studies Miller-Young (2014) found that there were performers who went into porn[5] specifically because of the creative aspects and how working in pornography was empowering, allowing them to make bold political statements about female pleasure. Griffith et al. (2012) also found similar themes that centered around those in porn being in a position to assist people in finding more sexual gratification in their lives and relationships.

In particular, Griffith et al. (2012) interviewed 176 porn actresses and approximately 10% of respondents answered "creative expression and personal growth" as to the reasons they chose porn as their profession. Case in point, adult performer and sex educator Nina Hartley declares, "I am sexual the way that Mozart was musical; life of public sexuality has, from my very first time on stage, been as natural to me as breathing" (Hartley, 2013, p. 228).

In my interviews, too, it was not uncommon to hear adult performers echo these themes as the reasons they went into pornography. An example of this was found in my interview with adult performer and entrepreneur, Alix Lovell, who underscored these ideas when she described to me how she got into pornography,

> ...I have always been a free spirit and I believe in sexual empowerment. We all need sex; it's like food and water. I like sex and now I happen to be getting paid for something I do anyway, but now I do it in a safer way. (Lovell, personal interview, February, 2019)

[5] Throughout this book the term *porn* will be the synecdoche for pornography.

Table 3.1 Responses of what adult performers liked about the adult entertainment industry

Category	*Frequency*	*Percentage*
Money	72	41
People	69	39
Sex	37	21
Freedom/Independence	32	18
Attention	23	13
Fun	14	8
Creative Expression	12	7
Personal Fulfillment	8	4
Rebellion	2	1

Source Adapted from Griffith et al. (2012)

Freelance writer Jarone Ashkenazi also found similar themes in interviews he conducted with porn stars[6] (Table 3.1); for example, Vicky Vette:

> I just wanted to be wild and crazy. I was living in a small town with small minds. I felt confined, restrained, constrained, restricted and repressed! I felt like I needed to break out. I was already criticized and penalized for the way I looked even when I dressed and acted conservatively. I was already a swinger, so it wasn't a stretch. I was done with the hypocrisy. (Ashkenazi, 2016, www.askmen.com/sex/sex_fantasies/why-women-go-into-porn.html)

In sum, money-as-motivator aside, workers in pornography, especially those considered "porn stars" align with what Jones, Lorenzen, and Sapsed (2015) put forth in how creative industries produce a peculiar type of individual success that is not simply rewarded financially: "We might call these individuals 'elite cultural producers', but in common parlance they are 'stars.' What distinguishes cultural stars from other industries (e.g., finance or technology) is that their public personae are valued in tandem with their skills" (p. 171). Presumably, the 13.3 million Instagram followers of porn star Sunny Leone would certainly concur.[7]

[6] The metonymy of "porn star" seems to be used for anyone still in the business for more than a year.

[7] https://www.dailydot.com/irl/instagram-porn-stars/.

Performance as an Instrument of Oppression

"All culture might be produced within a capitalist system, but it is pornography that is accused of exploiting its workers" (Simonton & Smith, 2004, p. 353). In this most provocative perspective, performance is viewed as a means of control and dehumanization. Here, the pornography performer is exploited, does not become rich, only the producers of pornography (often men) who have never appeared in front of the camera themselves (Szalai, 2010). Through this lens, individuals receive compensation, but as a pyrrhic victory subsequent to coercive and demanding behaviors.

This view is swiftly adopted by critics of pornography; none more vocal than anti-pornography campaigner feminist Gail Dines, a professor emerita of sociology and women's studies. Dines has dedicated much of her academic life conveying this view of pornography as harsh and degrading; porn is not just benign titillation (Dines, 2010), but a body-punishing spectacle (Jensen & Dines, 1998):

> It changes the way women and girls think about their bodies, their sexuality and their relationships. Every group that has fought for liberation understands that media images are part and parcel of the systematic dehumanization of an oppressed group. The more porn images filter into mainstream culture, the more girls and women are stripped of full human status and reduced to sex objects. This has a terrible effect on girls' sexual identity because it robs them of their own sexual desire. (Dines, as quoted in Bindel, 2018)

Even with such sustained feminist criticism, Cawston (2019) points out that the production of pornography does not show signs of waning; it pivots with the times and genre trends, and just reinvents itself. Sex workers appear to like their work, are excited about their work, and although may be members of a deviant group as defined by society, have a strong support system made up of like-minded individuals from within the sex work industry (Griffith, Capiola, & Gu, 2016).

Tool(s) of the Trade—Job Performance Aids

In HRM, job performance aids or *job aids* for short are a supplemental part of job performance, and are non-instructive interventions to improve job performance (Rossett & Schafer, 2006). Specifically, when added to the work situation, job aids are anything that improves job performance by guiding, facilitating, or reminding performers what to do in accomplishing job tasks (Chalupsky & Kopf, 1967); they take on many different forms: from checklists, how-to instructions, and laminated cards with phone extensions, to scale models and to-do lists (Sleight, 1993; Willmore, 2006). And, in the pornography industry their use is no exception. For example, according to adult film producer and director, Dan Leal, "Every man is on penis pill supplements or injections; you have to be, and any guy who says he isn't is lying. In the real world, you don't have sex for this long; that's the reality.[8]" Also, varied substances are used to aid in the production of imitation semen including Cetaphil lotion, egg whites, yogurt, and shampoo.[9] Perhaps not surprisingly, the pornography industry has led the way in performance sex aids, including in computer-controlled sex toys called "teledildonics" (Barss, 2011), sex robots, long-distance touch-transmitting gloves, couple's apps, and remote and app-controlled vibrators,[10] many of which were on display at the conventions I attended.

Performance Evaluation: So, What's the Difference Between a Good Sex Worker and a Bad One?

A significant part of performance management is centered around performance evaluation. At its core, a worker's performance—good or bad—does not just *happen*; in every work setting, including pornography production, performance is an outcome of three variables, viz.,: ability—the capacity of the employee to perform the job; collectively, the worker's knowledge, skills, and attitudes (KSAs)[11]; motivation—the worker's willingness to perform the job voluntarily; and the work environment—anything within the environment that would affect the worker's job performance (e.g., coworkers, poor lighting, pushy director). In sum, if a worker is not performing well, it is usually either she doesn't know

[8] http://fortune.com/2016/02/05/this-is-what-its-really-like-to-work-in-porn/.

[9] https://blogs.adultempire.com/2018/01/09/things-used-fake-cum-porn/.

[10] https://www.glamour.com/gallery/best-sex-tech-inventions-2017.

[11] A worker's competency framework is often referred to as knowledge, skills, and attitudes (KSAs) or collectively the worker's "ability" (Kopp, 2014).

how to do it, doesn't want to do it, or something is getting in her way from doing it well (Kopp, 2014).

In a traditional workplace, assessing an employee's performance often takes on the form of an annual performance review, which may or may not be linked to increased compensation. In the gig economy that is pornography—and common for independent contractors[12]—there are no formal performance appraisal systems, workers are typically paid by the hour or a day rate; adult performers are paid based on a flat rate per scene or photo shoot (Tarrant, 2016); formative or summative feedback is usually informal or incidental—"I step in if movements are weird or if there's not enough interaction with the camera" (Adult film director/producer Keith Moore as quoted by Tarrant, 2016, p. 37).

Evaluating the performance of those who work in pornography has both a proximal and a distal dimension. At a proximal level, like traditional employees, there are performance expectations of those who work in pornography: dependability, strong work ethic, good attitude, not acting like a diva, and flexibility (Bruckert & Parent, 2018; Miller-Young, 2014; Snow, 2016; Tarrant, 2016; Zeischegg & Wylde, 2018). Porn veteran Aurora Snow, "just like any other job, punctuality and preparation are necessary for long-term success. Showing up for work two or three hours late won't get a performer fired, but word spreads quickly" (Snow, 2016).[13]

Distally, and much like the traditional Nielsen ratings for television shows, analytics from social media provide another source of data about an adult performer's popularity (Tarrant, 2016). A performer's social media fan base is a metric tethered to potential sales performance and, as a result, producers of porn take an interest in adult performers branding on social media. As adult entertainment producer and director, Kevin Moore described,

[12] Classifying a worker as an employee or independent contractor is based on meeting certain criteria set out by the IRS. For example, an individual is considered an "employee" if the employer has the right to control work process. Likewise, an employment relationship exists if an individual is economically dependent on a business for continued employment. Organizations that misclassified workers as independent contractor risk fines and levies. Misclassifying employees as independent contractors and failing to provide W-2 forms can subject an employer to back taxes of as much as 41.5% of the contractors' wages, and these penalties can go back for three years (Cohen & Eimicke, 2013).

[13] https://fortune.com/2016/02/05/this-is-what-its-really-like-to-work-in-porn/.

> The top-tier performer pool can demand much higher pay. They can hurt a company's sales by refusing to shoot for them, because they have such a strong fan base. They use social media to both highly promote themselves or scene, but also call out any bad practices. The companies know they need these highly popular performers and will bend over backward for them. (Miller, 2014)

Ultimately, performance evaluation is used ultimately to gauge the amount of value added from a worker in terms of increased business revenue and the overall return on investment (ROI) (Kessler, 2019; McGovern & Gendron, 2017). And, today, it is through social media platforms such as Instagram, Facebook, YouTube, and Twitter that adult performers become part of that top-tier pool (Marwick, 2013; Miller, 2014).

References

Agustin, L. M. (2005). New research directions: The cultural study of commercial sex. *Sexualities, 8*(5), 618–631. https://doi.org/10.1177/1363460705058400.

Alagaraja, M. (2012). HRD and HRM perspectives on organizational performance: A review of literature. *Human Resource Development Review, 12*(2), 117–143.

Amabile, T., & Kramer, S. (2013). *The progress principle: Using small wins to ignite joy, engagement, and creativity at work*. New York: Perseus Books Group.

Anderson, N., Ones, D. S., Sinangil, H. K., & Viswesvaran, C. (2001). *Handbook of industrial, work & organizational psychology: Volume 1: Personnel psychology*. Thousand Oaks, CA: Sage.

Armstrong, S., & Appelbaum, M. (2003). *Stress-free performance appraisals: Turn your most painful management duty into a powerful motivational tool*. Franklin Lakes, NJ: Career Press.

Ashkenazi, J. (2016). *Why women go into porn: Four adult film stars revealed why they really chose XXX*. Retrieved from https://www.askmen.com/sex/sex_fantasies/why-women-go-into-porn.html.

Bali, A. (2015). Psychological factors affecting sports performance. *International Journal of Physical Education, 1*(6), 92–95.

Bandura, A. (1977). *Social learning theory*. Englewood Cliffs, NJ: Prentice Hall.

Barss, P. (2011). *The erotic engine: How pornography has powered mass communication from Gutenberg to Google*. Toronto: Anchor Canada.

Bindel, J. (2018). The truth about the porn industry. *The Guardian*. Retrieved from https://www.theguardian.com/lifeandstyle/2010/jul/02/gail-dines-pornography.

Bruckert, C., & Parent, C. (2018). *Getting past 'the pimp': Management in the sex industry*. Toronto: University of Toronto Press.

Cawston, A. (2019). The feminist case against pornography: A review and re-evaluation. *Inquiry, 62*(6), 624–658. https://doi.org/10.1080/0020174X.2018.1487882.

Chalupsky, A. B., & Kopf, T. J. (1967). *Job performance aids and their impact on manpower utilization*. Palo Alto, CA: Philco-Ford Corporation.

Cohen, S., & Eimicke, W. (2013). *Independent contracting: Policy and management analysis*. New York: Columbia University.

Dines, G. (2010). *Pornland: How porn has hijacked our sexuality*. Boston: Beacon Press.

Fleishman, E. A. (1954). Dimensional analysis of psychomotor abilities. *Journal of Experimental Psychology, 48*(6), 437–454. https://doi.org/10.1037/h0058244.

Gagné, M., & Deci, E. L. (2005). Self-determination theory and work motivation. *Journal of Organizational Behavior, 26*(4), 331–362.

Gini, A. (1998). Work, identity and self: How we are formed by the work we do. *Journal of Business Ethics, 17*(7), 707–714.

Griffith, J. D., Adams, L., Hart, C., & Mitchell, S. (2012). Why become a pornography actress? *International Journal of Sexual Health, 24*, 165–180.

Griffith, J. D., Capiola, A., & Gu, L. (2016). The career development of bisexual sex workers. In T. Köllen (Ed.), *Sexual orientation and transgender issues in organizations: Global perspectives on LGBT workforce diversity* (pp. 353–366). Cham: Springer International Publishing.

Hartley, N. (Ed.). (2013). *Porn: An effective vehicle for sexual role modeling and education*. New York, NY: Feminist Press.

Jensen, R., & Dines, G. (1998). The content of mass-marketed pornography. In G. Dines, R. Jensen, & A. Russo (Eds.), *Pornography: The production and consumption of inequality* (pp. 65–100). New York and London: Routledge.

Jones, C., Lorenzen, M., & Sapsed, J. (2015). *The Oxford handbook of creative industries*. Oxford: Oxford University Press.

Kessler, S. (2019). *Gigged: The gig economy, the end of the job and the future of work*. London: Penguin Random House.

Kopp, D. M. (2014). *HRD: Performance through learning*. San Diego, CA: Bridgepoint.

Lee, J., & Sullivan, R. (2016). Porn and labour: The labour of porn studies. *Porn Studies, 3*(2), 104–106. London: Taylor & Francis.

Marwick, A. E. (2013). *Status update: Celebrity, publicity, and branding in the social media age*. New Haven: Yale University Press.

Maslow, A. H. (1943). A theory of human motivation. *Psychological Review, 50*(4), 370–396.

McGovern, M., & Gendron, G. (2017). *Thriving in the gig economy: How to capitalize and compete in the new world of work.* Newburyport: Red Wheel Weiser.

McKee, A. (2016). Pornography as a creative industry: Challenging the exceptionalist approach to pornography. *Porn Studies, 3*(2), 107–119. https://doi.org/10.1080/23268743.2015.1065202.

Miller, A. (2014). Confessions of a pornographer! Interview with Kevin Moore. *Something Awful.* Retrieved from https://www.somethingawful.com/comedy-goldmine/kevin-moore-porn/5/.

Miller-Young, M. (2014). *A taste for brown sugar: Black Women in pornography.* Duke: Duke University Press.

Rossett, A., & Schafer, L. (2006). *Job aids and performance support: Moving knowledge in the classroom to knowledge everywhere.* San Francisco: Wiley.

Rousseau, D. M. (1989). Psychological and implied contracts in organizations. *Employee Responsibilities and Rights Journal, 2,* 121–139.

Rummler, G., & Brache, A. (1995). *Improving performance: How to manage the white space on the organization chart* (2nd ed.). San Francisco: Jossey-Bass.

Simonton, A., & Smith, C. (2004). Who are women in pornography? In C. Stark & R. Whisnant (Eds.), *Not for sale: Feminists resisting prostitution and pornography* (pp. 352–361). Melbourne: Spinifex.

Sleight, D. A. (1993). *A developmental history of training in the United States and europe.* Lansing: Michigan State University.

Snow, A. (2016, May 2). This is what it's really like to work in porn. *Fortune.*

Swanson, R. A. (1995). Human resource development: Performance is the key. *Human Resource Development Quarterly, 6*(2), 207–213.

Swanson, R. A., & Holton, E. F. (2009). *Foundations of human resource development.* Scotts Valley: Createspace Independent Pub.

Szalai, G. (2010). Vivid. A new business model for porn. *The Hollywood Reporter.* Retrieved from http://www.hollywoodreporter.com/news/vivid-new-business-model-porn-27414.

Tarrant, S. (2016). *The pornography industry: What everyone needs to know.* Oxford: Oxford University Press.

Weiss, H. M. (2013). Working as human nature. In J. Ford, R. Hollenbeck, & A. Ryan (Eds.), *The nature of work* (pp. 35–48). Washington, DC: American Psychological Association.

Williams, R. S. (1998). *Performance management: Perspectives on employee performance.* London: International Thomson Business Press.

Willmore, J. (2006). *Job aids basics.* Alexandria: ASTD Press.

Zeischegg, C., & Wylde, D. (2018). *Body to job.* Los Angeles: Rare Bird Books.

CHAPTER 4

Career Development

Abstract In this chapter, career management and development aspects will be explored. Length of tenure, job enlargement, and job enrichment are discussed. Also, how many workers in pornography endeavor to leave performing and go back to "normal" life. Some performers become producers and directors in the adult film business, as well as, start their own pornography companies. Others try to go onto mainstream movies and entertainment like Jenna Jameson and Traci Lords. Explored also is how mainstream celebrities became more popular or discovered because of the release of a sex tape. Examples of this are with Pamela Anderson and Tommy Lee, Montana Fishburne and in the case of Kim Kardashian, a sex tape led to an empire.

Keywords Career development · Protean · KSAs · Job enlargement · Job enrichment · Career management

A Career in Pornography—Protean and Boundaryless

Career management and development, sometimes referred to as talent management, is an important and generative part to HRM practice and supports the worker after he or she is recruited and selected. Once in the trade, like customary employees, workers in pornography go through

D. M. Kopp, *Human Resource Management in the Pornography Industry*, https://doi.org/10.1007/978-3-030-37659-8_4

similar, if highly compacted phases in their career—a sequential process that starts from an understanding of oneself and encompasses occupational awareness (Hall, 2002; Pulkkinen, Ohranen, & Tolvanen, 1999). Generally, there are five career stages (Werner & DeSimone, 2011) to career management:

> 1) preparation for the work, a stage where the workers must acquire the knowledge, skills, and attitudes (KSAs) they will need to enter the career; 2) entry into the organization, here the worker considers job offers and selects the appropriate company; 3) fitting into the chosen occupation, learning the rules and norms; 4) reappraisal of career choice and goodness of fit; and, 5) preparing for and effective retirement from the career.

Usually, within a company-employee setting, career development involves the organization leading an assessment of the employee. One methodology that arose in the early 1970s was the GE–McKinsey nine-box framework (Fig. 4.1), following on the heels of the Boston Consulting Group's well-known growth share matrix (Couch & Citrin, 2019). In this matrix, two dimensions of the worker are evaluated—performance and potential, which may dictate the employee's future advancement in an organization. Within the gig economy that is pornography, however, it is the sex worker, not the organization, who self-directedly manages and takes the responsibility for his or her own career development and employability, known as a protean career (Hall, 2002; Korunka & Kubicek, 2017). As well, unlike the typical employee, but consistent with the gig worker, the adult performer is not bounded to particular organizations, but works in a trade that moves across the boundaries of separate gig employers, what Arthur and Rousseau (2001) referred to as the "boundaryless career."

And, consider, too, like the dynamic present in today's conventional workforce, the pornography industry, too, for the first time has up to five generations of adult performer represented and working together (Zemke, Raines, & Filipczak, 2013).

- Traditionalists—born before 1946 (e.g., "Granny porn")
- Baby Boomers—born between 1946 and 1964 ("GILF")
- Generation X—born between 1965 and 1976 ("MILF")
- Generation Y, or Millennials—born between 1977 and 1997
- Generation Z—born after 1997.

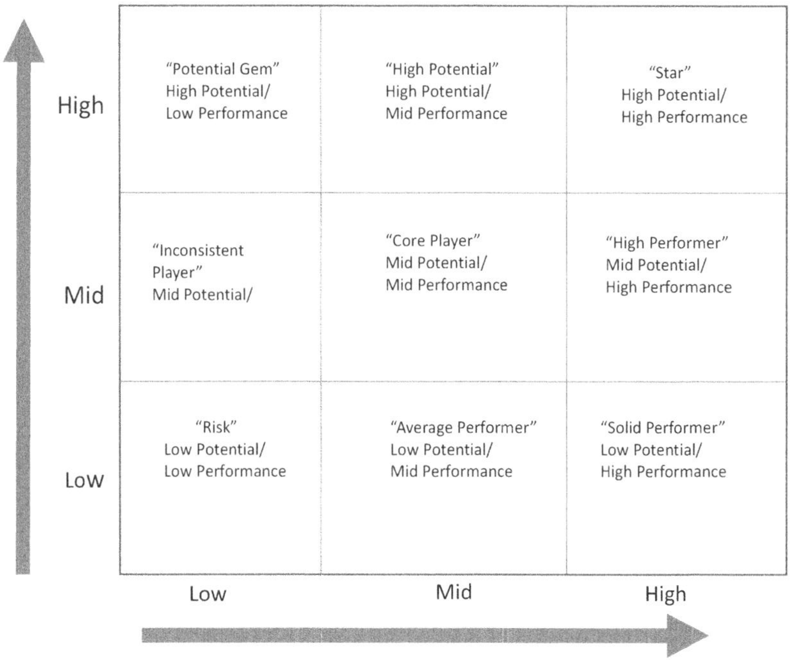

Fig. 4.1 Talent development model (*Source* Adapted from Bersin & Chamorro-Premuzic, 2019)

Porn Career Antecedents

There are many variables as to why someone chooses to go into a profession (Pulkkinen, Ohranen, & Tolvanen, 1999). As previously discussed, based on a study by Griffith, Adams, Hart, and Mitchell (2012) of female performers in the adult entertainment industry, the main reason for choosing the pornography industry was the money, followed by the sex and the attention (Table 4.1).

This was corroborated with my field interviews with adult performers where each stressed how—especially in the face of their accrued "college debt," for example—pornography offered a way to counter the financial obligations and responsibilities.

The need for money included, what Tarrant (2016) called *survival sex work* that is performed for immediate, primary needs such as food,

Table 4.1 Frequencies and percentages of why women went into pornography

Category	*Frequency*	*Percentage*
Money	94	53
Sex	48	27
Attention	29	16
Fun	20	11
Related industry	12	7
Acquaintance	13	7
Chance	11	6
Creative expression	9	5
Personal growth	8	4
Disliked prior job	8	4

Source Adapted from Griffith et al. (2012)

clothing, shelter; such was somberly displayed in the documentary *Hot Girls Wanted* (2015) that followed young women who enter the porn industry without previous experience to be a part of porn production for the amateur adult website market. This documentary shows a dark and unsavory side of the sex-work industry.

Yet, a subsequent study by Griffith et al. (2013) upended what was thought to be the long-established reason why female performers got into porn—the "damaged goods" theory. The damaged goods theory puts forth that performers in the adult entertainment industry have higher rates of childhood sexual abuse, psychological problems, and drug use compared to the typical woman. In Griffith's subsequent study, while female performers were more likely to have used more types of drugs compared to the comparison group, in terms of psychological characteristics, porn actresses, in fact, had higher levels of self-esteem, positive feelings, social support, sexual satisfaction, and spirituality compared to the matched group (p. 621). In sum, the findings did not provide support for the damaged goods theory.

Career Management—Job Enlargement and Job Enrichment

While the sex worker is a gig worker, perhaps unlike other gig workers, workers in porn are faced with a particular career precarity; that is, a career made more precarious due to environmental conditions ranging from unaccommodating independent contractor laws to formal and informal anti-sex worker codes (Berg & Penley, 2016). Women and men performers in porn have very different paths when it comes to career longevity (Tibbals & Flynt, 2015). The vast majority of women come in and out of the industry in a few months to a few years; for males, the average duration of a career in pornography is around five years (Ketcham, 2012). Yet, even with a career precarity backdrop, adult performers, like mainstream employees, move through their careers by diversifying and employ aspects of job enrichment and job enlargement.

Job enrichment are vertical stretch assignments and opportunities that expose workers to deeper dimensions of their own job (Werner & DeSimone, 2011). In the case of pornography, it may be the undertaking of new types of sex on camera like anal sex or entering another genre. For example, a first time performing on camera with a trans-sexual partner or in a lesbian scene. Efforts in job enrichment may be tied to the attraction of extra compensation for doing a scene considered rarer or taboo.

Job enlargement, sometimes called horizontal development, is an opportunity that allows employees to get a better appreciation of the larger picture and the interrelationships of differ-ent jobs (Werner & DeSimone, 2011). In pornography, this may take on the form of an adult performer, in addition to performing in film, moving into producing or directing pornography, as well. This movement from in front of the camera to behind the camera is an example of job enlargement. Consider the example of former porn star Asia Carrera, who enjoyed learning all the crew members' jobs in between her scenes (Tarrant, 2016; Wagoner, 2010).

Post Porn Career

Typical of gig workers, a career development strategy may be non-existent if not scant with a compressed timeline (Kessler, 2019; McGovern & Gendron, 2017), which aligns to the tenure of the average adult performer, which is only around one year according to Mark Spiegler, talent agent for pornographic actresses[1] (M. Spiegler, personal interview, February, 2019). To the extent adult performers utilized the pornography industry to earn and save money, some return to their non-porn

[1] Spiegler is founder of Spiegler Girls (often regarded as being among the adult film industry's top agencies).

career trajectories, with many finishing their college degrees.[2] Some move behind the scenes writing scripts, directing, or becoming makeup artists (Tarrant, 2016, p. 68).

Michelle Sinclair, formerly known as porn star Belladonna described her post porn career

> Since I retired three years ago it's been a trip. I don't know if it's like this for any other girl who leaves the adult industry, but for me, I'm trying to find myself. ... I've thought about the sex-positive speaker route but I've also thought about a lot of things ... I feel like I'm at the place where most people are when they're just out of college, or getting ready to go to college, and figuring out what it is they really want to do with their lives." Still, she says, "I don't want to be typecast and I don't want to be naked, which is what most people would want to cast me for in mainstream films. (Nieratko, 2015)

As many former adult performers go back into a conventional life where friends and extended family may or may not know about their careers in pornography, there are varied outcomes. In his documentary, "After Porn Ends," a film that looks at the lives of real people who found their way in and out of the pornographic industry, film student Bryce Wagoner interviewed former porn stars who landed into ordinariness—a stay-at-home mom, a bounty hunter, a writer and other inherently normal citizens "starring in the leading roles of everyday life" (Wagoner, 2010).

It may have been invisible to some that these individuals were once stars in the adult entertainment industry; however, Wagoner found the stigma remained when the former was known:

> While men stayed in the business as long as they could and were most okay with it...every woman we spoke to, apart from Amber Lynn, who is still going strong, had to reboot her life at 30 and start over in some small town. We found many stories where people tried to move on only for their neighbors to find out that they once made a bunch of dirty movies. One guy couldn't coach his son's little league team anymore. One woman

[2] Research, which involved interviews with 300 exotic dancers, found there was a high level of job satisfaction and all had some qualifications. A quarter had degrees, while one in three women were in some form of education, with about 14% working to fund an undergraduate course and about 6% to fund a postgraduate degree (https://www.reuters.com/article/us-britain-lapdancing/study-finds-quarter-of-uk-lap-dancers-have-degrees-idUSTRE67Q2YW20100827).

> lost her real-estate job. The late male porn start John Leslie wasn't able to babysit when neighbors found out about his past. (Thompson & Gibbs, 2016, p. 278)

As mentioned, some workers in pornography leave performing to become producers and directors in the adult film business, as well as, start their own pornography companies, some adult performers are, indeed, able to break into mainstream movies and entertainment like porn veterans Jenna Jameson, Traci Lords, and even Ron Jeremy, perhaps the most famous male in porn who still cameos into the mainstream, but this is statistically rare (Kalenda, 2016; Rose, 2013; Tarrant, 2016; Voss, 2015).[3]

Ironically, whereas mainstream celebrities became discovered or become even more popular because of the release of a sex tape—examples including Pamela Anderson and Tommy Lee, Paris Hilton and in the case of Kim Kardashian, a sex tape led to an empire—that dynamic has proven not to be bi-directional for workers in pornography.[4]

Post-modern Porn Career

At the XBIZ conference I attended in Miami, I had a very fascinating conversation with a man from an Augmented Reality (AR) company; this technology is becoming very popular in pornography with apps already created and available for smartphones. Augmented reality and virtual reality are inverse reflections of one in another; that is, virtual reality (VR) offers a digital recreation of a real-life setting, while augmented reality (AR) delivers virtual elements as an overlay to the real world. Specifically, users watch, interact and can live out sexual fantasies with life-sized erotic virtual holograms in the real-world; applications allow you to watch and participate in sex acts with 3D virtual avatars of popular porn stars in the real-world.

As was explained to me, virtual reality porn is just foreplay, but augmented reality is the future of adult entertainment. I began to reflect

[3] Former porn star, Mary Carey ran for governor of California twice, promising to legalize gay marriage and tax breast implants (Kalenda, 2016).

[4] Even Former Disney star Bella Thorne recently stepped out of mainstream to direct her first porn film. The 21-year-old actress has partnered with Pornhub to release "Her & Him," a film part of the porn site's Visionaries Director's Series. https://www.foxnews.com/entertainment/bella-thorne-director-porn-film.

how while sex between sequestered consenting adults has been more or less unchanged for 50,000 years (Buss, 2003); the modalities for those who would watch consenting adults have sex has changed greatly. It raises not only questions regarding the future of pornography, but also what exactly will a career in pornography be in the future?

References

Arthur, M. B., & Rousseau, D. M. (2001). *The boundaryless career: A new employment principle for a new organizational era*. New York, NY: Oxford University Press.

Berg, H., & Penley, C. (2016). Creative precarity in the adult film industry. In M. Curtin & K. Sanson (Eds.), *Precarious creativity* (pp. 159–171). Berkeley: University of California Press.

Bersin, J., & Chamorro-Premuzic, T. (2019). New ways to gauge talent and potential. *MIT Sloan Management Review, 60*(2), 1.

Buss, D. M. (2003). *The evolution of desire: Strategies of human mating*. New York: Basic Books.

Couch, M. A., & Citrin, R. S. (2019). *Strategy-driven leadership: The playbook for developing your next generation of leaders*. New York: Taylor & Francis.

Griffith, J. D., Adams, L., Hart, C., & Mitchell, S. (2012). Why become a pornography actress? *International Journal of Sexual Health, 24,* 165–180.

Griffith, J. D., Mitchell, S., Hart, C. L., Adams, L. T., & Gu, L. L. (2013). Pornography actresses: An assessment of the damaged goods hypothesis. *The Journal of Sex Research, 50*(7), 621–632. https://doi.org/10.1080/00224499.2012.719168.

Hall, D. T. (2002). *Careers in and out of organizations*. Thousand Oaks, CA: Sage.

Kalenda, J. (2016). Pornography as part of the socio-cultural changes in Kubátová. In H. Kubátová, K. Čada, M. Fafejta, I. Chorvát, K. Ivanová, E. Jarošová, J. Kalenda, L. Křeménková, D. Lužný, & E. Moravčíková (Eds.), *Ways of Life in the Late Modernity*. Czech Republic: Univerzita Palackého v Olomouci.

Kessler, S. (2019). *Gigged: The gig economy, the end of the job and the future of work*. New York: Penguin Random House.

Ketcham, J. (2012). *I am Jennie*. New York: Gallery Books.

Korunka, C., & Kubicek, B. (2017). *Job demands in a changing world of work: Impact on workers' health and performance and implications for research and practice*. Cham, Switzerland: Springer.

McGovern, M., & Gendron, G. (2017). *Thriving in the gig economy: How to capitalize and compete in the new world of work*. Red Wheel Weiser.

Nieratko, C. (2015). Catching up with the actress formerly known as Belladonna. *VICE*.

Pulkkinen, L., Ohranen, M., & Tolvanen, A. (1999). Personality antecedents of career orientation and stability among women compared to men. *Journal of Vocational Behavior, 54*(1), 37–58. https://doi.org/10.1006/jvbe.1998.1653.

Rose, D. (2013). *The ethics and politics of pornography*. London, UK: Palgrave Macmillan.

Tarrant, S. (2016). *The pornography industry: What everyone needs to know*. New York, NY: Oxford University Press.

Thompson, W. E., & Gibbs, J. C. (2016). *Deviance and deviants: A sociological approach*. Hoboken: Wiley.

Tibbals, C., & Flynt, T. (2015). *Exposure: A sociologist explores sex, society, and adult entertainment*. Austin: Greenleaf Book Group Press.

Voss, G. (2012). Treating it as a normal business: Researching the pornography industry. *Sexualities, 15*(3/4), 391–410. https://doi.org/10.1177/1363460712439650.

Voss, G. (2015). *Stigma and the shaping of the pornography industry*. Taylor & Francis.

Wagoner, B. (Writer). (2010). *After porn ends*. Eastern Carolina University.

Werner, J. M., & DeSimone, R. L. (2011). *Human resource development*. Mason, OH: Cengage Learning.

Zemke, R., Raines, C., & Filipczak, B. (2013). *Generations at work: Managing the clash of boomers, Gen Xers, and Gen Yers in the workplace*. New York: AMACOM.

CHAPTER 5

Workforce Diversity

Abstract In this chapter, the author investigates the state of diversity in the pornography workplace. According to Flory (2015), the pornography industry has a diversity problem. This hierarchy usually proceeds according to which sex acts are considered most taboo and, sometimes, most physically demanding for the female performer. However, "interracial" porn, which is frequently seen as the ultimate feat for an actress, is held out as more extreme not because of which body part goes where, but because the adult industry reflects the old attitude society still holds on to: that the color of a sexual partner's skin can by itself make the act forbidden. The author explores the state of diversity and biases in pornography industry.

Keywords Workplace diversity · Inclusion · Title VII · Assimilation · Interracial

To be sure, workplace diversity as aspirational and salutary is widely accepted and a well-established goal within the field of human resource management today. Indeed, achieving, maintaining, and managing a diverse workforce at the strategic, tactical and operational levels is part of most strategic human resource plans (Ely & Thomas, 2001; Joseph & Selvaraj, 2015; Page, 2008; Shena, Ashok, D'Nettob, & Mongaa, 2009).

D. M. Kopp, *Human Resource Management in the Pornography Industry*, https://doi.org/10.1007/978-3-030-37659-8_5

Workplace diversity refers broadly to the differences between and among workers that include race, religion, gender, age, cultural background, disabilities, and sexual orientation; even deeper diversity dimensions were posited by Loden and Rosener in their "diversity wheel," including more subtle elements such as the individual's socio-economic stratification, union affiliation, education level and parental status (Loden & Rosener, 1991). In fact, today's American workforce is as diverse than ever,[1] buoyed perhaps by such rhetorical refrains as Steven Covey's, "Strength lies in differences, not in similarities" (Covey, 2004).

Over the last three decades, research on the potential and promise of a diverse workplace—especially as a potent performance driver—has abounded. Specifically, a robust workplace diversity program is said to engender better quality decision-making (Galinsky et al., 2015), a deeper level of innovation (Bersin & Chamorro-Premuzic, 2019), improved team performance (Barta, Kleiner, & Neumann, 2012; Eagly & Wood, 1991; Joseph & Selvaraj, 2015; Page, 2008; Shore et al., 2011), and other enhanced bottom-line metrics (Carrell, Mann, & Tracey, 2006; Ely & Thomas, 2001; Tatli & Ozbilgin, 2009; Wood, 1987). Today, a Google search of the phrase "benefits of workplace diversity" yields over 41,000 results.[2]

Thomas and Ely introduced three fundamental paradigms that classify an organization's motivation and rationale for pursuing workforce diversity (Ely & Thomas, 2001; Thomas & Ely, 1996):

- Discrimination and Fairness,
- Access and Legitimacy, and
- Integration and Learning.

While these concepts do not neatly operationalize themselves within the pornography industry, they are worth discussing, nevertheless.

The Discrimination and Fairness perspective of workplace diversity is rooted in the notion that an organization practices workplace diversity

[1] According to the National Center for Public Policy and Higher Education, from 1980 to 2020, the white working-age population is projected to decline from 82% to 63%. During the same period, the minority portion of the workforce is projected to double (from 18% to 37%), and the Hispanic/Latino portion is projected to almost triple (from 6 to 17%). http://www.highereducation.org/reports/pa_decline/decline-f1.shtml

[2] As of September, 2019.

from a lens of legal compliance vis-à-vis Title VII of the Civil Rights Act of 1964, the U.S. federal law that prohibits employers from discriminating against employees on the basis of sex, race, color, national origin and religion,[3] and it generally applies to employers with 15 or more employees, including federal, state and local governments; here diversity practices are driven by a commitment to Affirmative Action (AA) and Equal Employment Opportunity (EEO) (Shena et al., 2009). Admittedly, because most performers in pornography are classified as independent contractors, they would not be afforded the protections under Title VII (Horne, Williamson, & Herman, 2018); however, this classification may be changing. In September of 2019, California governor Gavin Newsom signed Assembly Bill 5, the state's rewritten employment law, much of the focus was on Uber and Lyft drivers. Yet, under this law, performers in the adult entertainment industry, too, would be entitled to the same benefits as those drivers, specifically being recognized as employees of the companies they work for. This would give the porn worker the right to overtime pay, minimum wage protection and workers' compensation protections, as well as, presumably, the shelter of Title VII.

The Access and Legitimacy perspective of workplace diversity motivates organizations to implement diversity practices not only from a compliance standpoint, but also because they believe it makes business sense to do so; the so-called business case for diversity. Accordingly, this business case for workplace diversity rests on the premise that demographically mixed groups can leverage their differences to be more resourceful and productive (Carrell et al., 2006; Ely & Thomas, 2001; Tatli & Ozbilgin, 2009; Wood, 1987)[4]; as a result, performance and, therefore, a company's bottom line and competitive advantage, can be improved. To be sure, a case could be made that the pornography industry produces its production of interracial pornography (IR) because it makes business

[3] Title VII does not explicitly address employment discrimination based on sexual orientation or gender identity

[4] The promise of workplace diversity is not without its critics, however. According to Maitland (2018) and McMahon (2010) prior, while there may be a business case to be made for workplace diversity, the evidence is usually tethered to the aspects and synergies found in *job-related* diversity, not *demographic* diversity; in sum, Maitland argues that the so-called benefits of workplace diversity may be down to "political sloganeering" Eagly (2016), too, found that the research findings on the benefits of workplace diversity are mixed, and repeated meta-analyses have yielded average correlational findings that were null or extremely small.

sense to do so. According to Snow (2018), the "interracial" genre in adult entertainment has been a consistent hit with consumers.

The third organizational perspective in workplace diversity is the Integration and Learning view; here, organizations not only acknowledge that diversity makes business sense, but leverage workplace diversity to aspire to become what Senge (2010) called "learning organizations," whose workforce operate under a shared vision, expertise-seeking, dialogue, systems thinking, and team learning, all necessary components for fundamental to organizational sustainability (Brown, 2017; Soyka, 2012). Interestingly, in the spirit of a learning organization, many note how pornography has driven the new technology. From interactive motion-controlled porn, sexual avatars, Internet cash transactions, virtual worlds and lobbying for anti-piracy legislation the adult industry broadens the commercialization of new technologies (Barss, 2011).

Workplace Diversity in the Pornography Industry: Inclusion on Their Terms

Statistically, but not necessarily owing to any targeted, the pornography industry itself already realizes a diverse workforce, essentially reflecting the demographics of the United States—70.5% Caucasian, 14% black, 9.3% Latin, 5.2% Asian, and 1% other (Millward, 2013).

Ironically, the business case for workplace diversity in the pornography industry is not due to demographically mixed groups leveraging their differences to be more creative and productive, but in utilizing racial (and racist) stereotypes to commodify and monetize sexual labor.[5]

It serves us well, therefore, to explore, not the de facto existence of workplace diversity in the pornography industry, but rather the richer construct of worker *inclusion*. Whereas workplace diversity is binary, inclusion is an active construct, a hypernym for belongingness and uniqueness (Hewlett, Rashid, & Sherbin, 2017; Shore et al., 2011).

A worker can only experience inclusion when he or she is thought of as both an insider as part of the in-group (high belongingness), as

[5] I experienced a similar dynamic during research in the social history of training. Some of the research addressed how many salespeople, as late as the 1930s, were trained in the so-called folk science of physiognomy—the notion that a person's outer appearance, especially the face, could provide insight into his or her true character or personality (Kopp & Desiderio, 2009).

well as allowed and/or encouraged to retain his or her individuality within the work group or organization (high uniqueness).[6] This dynamic makes inclusion more generative than normal *assimilation*, for example. While assimilation is necessary, it is not sufficient in making workers feel accepted and valued; an assimilated worker is treated as an insider, yet he or she downplays (or are given social cues to downplay) his or her uniqueness and conform. Distinguished diversity advocate Verna Myers posited this way, "If diversity is being invited to the party, then inclusion is being asked to dance" (Myers, 2013); if we extrapolate this as it relates to the pornography industry, it may be something similar to, if diversity is the ability for anyone being able to join the porn industry, then inclusion is when they are asked [by producers] to have sex in videos.

Inclusive organizational cultures are said to maximize business outcomes by engendering innovation, deeper worker engagement, and highly effective teams (Brown, 2017; Engelmeier, 2018). And, particularly, members of a stigma group are more cohesive. Ashforth and Kreiner proposed that morally stigmatized dirty workers are more likely (than members of physically or socially tainted occupations) to rely on the collective or other occupational members as sources of social validation, thus reducing feelings of stigma (Ashforth & Kreiner, 1999).

"Lotus Blossom" or "Dragon Lady"[7]—On the |Absolute Value| of the Double Bind

Thus, the overarching inquiry becomes: Can workers in the pornography industry who are utilized as stereotypes still experience inclusion? This inquiry challenges the dynamic of *stereotype threat* where, in traditional

[6] Due to the recent popularity of pornography featuring transgender women, the transgender community is finding employment in the adult film industry. Searches for the word transgender have gone up by nearly 300 percent over the past three years on the Pornhub website alone (Role, 2017). Likewise, a Google video search of "Disabled Women in Porn" renders an astounding 55 million results!

[7] Zhou and Paul (2016) undertook a content analysis to consider the depiction of sexual behaviors in a random sample of videos from the "Asian Women" category of content. The study showed that women in the Asian women category were depicted very differently from women in other categories of pornography. Women in Asian women category of pornography were treated less aggressively. In addition, women in Asian women category were less objectified but also had lower agency in sexual activities. Thus, the Asian women stereotype in current pornography is closer to "Lotus Blossom" and far away from "Dragon Lady". https://link.springer.com/article/10.1007/S12119-016-9375-9.

organizations, negatively stereotyped persons underperform (Walton, Murphy, & Ryan, 2105) when up against their non-minority counterparts. In fact, colorblindness and stereotype threat are barriers to inclusion (Casad & Bryant, 2016; Markus, Steele, & Steele, 2000).

In principle, one can make a complicated point that minority performers in the pornography industry would experience inclusion because they are not only considered an integral part of the in-group, but also their unique physicality is celebrated (albeit, in a perverse way), supporting psychologist Marty Klein's point about the myth of racist pornography (Klein, 2012).

In her book, *A Taste for Brown Sugar: Black Women in Pornography*, Mirelle Miller-Young suggested that those who would take part of commodifying sexuality do not necessarily resist hegemonic institutions of power including racial capitalism; they are wont to accommodate the "incapacities of profit-seeking system" (Miller-Young, 2014, p. 235). Activist and social critic Gail Dines goes further to proclaim pornography's double-standard as it relates to allowance of racism in porn,

> (P)ornography is used as a vehicle to transmit messages about the legitimacy of racism and sexism. Hiding behind the facade of fantasy and harmless fun, pornography delivers reactionary racist stereotypes that would be considered unacceptable were they in any other types of mass-produced media. (Dines, 2020, https://fightthenewdrug.org/porn-industry-thrives-on-promoting-racism/)

Yet, Professor James Young makes the counterpoint that, even when profoundly offensive, the freedom of artistic expression must be upheld—that is, an artist's freedom to create is above their moral responsibility (Young, 2005), perhaps this is especially true of psychomotor expression versus cognitive or affective such as in pornography.

Notwithstanding, according to Flory (2015), the pornography industry has a diversity problem.[8] Flory posits that interracial porn, which is frequently seen as the ultimate feat for an actress, is held out as more extreme not because of which body part goes where, but because the adult industry reflects the old attitude society still holds on to: that the

[8] http://www.businessinsider.com/pornography-has-a-big-race-problem-2015-9.

color of a sexual partner's skin can by itself make the act forbidden.[9] Flory's point seems to be taken when considering the tweet put out by porn company Pornhub in 2014 for Martin Luther King Day encouraging users to only use the "Ebony" category for the occasion.

As it relates to workplace diversity in the pornography industry, mainstream pornography does exploit many racist stereotypes, but as perhaps an honest reflection of our cultural baggage (Flory, 2015). "Everything is put on the performers to be held morally responsible — thing is, porn is a fast-food model. We wouldn't make the things if people weren't buying the things," declares porn performer Mickey Mod (as cited by Flory, 2015).

Indeed, if the test of a first-rate intelligence is the ability to hold two opposing ideas in mind at the same time and, yet, still retain the ability to function,[10] then minority performers in porn, particularly, are no doubt gifted.

References

Ashforth, B., & Kreiner, G. (1999). How can you do it?: Dirty work and the challenge of constructing a positive identity. *The Academy of Management Review, 24*(3), 413–434.

Barss, P. (2011). *The erotic engine: How pornography has powered mass communication from Gutenberg to Google*. Toronto: Anchor Canada.

Barta, T., Kleiner, M., & Neumann, T. (2012). *Is there a payoff from top-team diversity?* Retrieved from https://www.mckinsey.com/business-functions/organization/our-insights/is-there-a-payoff-from-top-team-diversity.

Bernardi, D. (2007). Racism and pornography: Evidence, paradigms, and publishing. *Cinema Journal, 46*(4), 116–121.

Bersin, J., & Chamorro-Premuzic, T. (2019). New ways to gauge talent and potential. *MIT Sloan Management Review, 60*(2), 1.

Brooks, S. (2010). Hypersexualization and the dark body: Race and inequality among black and Latina women in the exotic dance industry. *Sexuality Research and Social Policy, 7*(2), 70–80. https://doi.org/10.1007/s13178-010-0010-5.

[9] And, according to (Landes & Nielsen, 2018), the practice of racial dodging is endemic in the porn industry. It mostly takes place when Caucasian female performers refuse to shoot scenes with African American male performers.

[10] As first quoted by F. Scott Fitzgerald (1936) in "The Crack Up".

Brown, J. (2017). *Inclusion: Diversity, the new workplace & the will to change*. Hartford: Publish Your Purpose Press.

Carrell, M. R., Mann, E. E., & Tracey, H. S. (2006). Defining workforce diversity programs and practices in organizations: A longitudinal study. *Labor Law Journal, 51*(1), 5–12.

Casad, B. J., & Bryant, W. J. (2016). Addressing stereotype threat is critical to diversity and inclusion in organizational psychology. *Frontiers in Psychology, 7*, 8. https://doi.org/10.3389/fpsyg.2016.00008.

Covey, S. R. (2004). *The 7 habits of highly effective people: Powerful lessons in personal change*. New York: Free Press.

Dines, G. (2020). *How the porn industry capitalizes off of racism and racist stereotypes*. Retrieved from https://fightthenewdrug.org/porn-industry-thrives-on-promoting-racism/.

Eagly, A. H. (2016). When passionate advocates meet research on diversity, does the honest broker stand a chance? *Journal of Social Issues, 72*(1), 199–222.

Eagly, A. H., & Wood, W. (1991). Explaining sex differences in social behavior: A meta-analytic perspective. *Personality and Social Psychology Bulletin, 17*(3), 306–315. https://doi.org/10.1177/0146167291173011.

Ely, R. J., & Thomas, D. A. (2001). Cultural diversity at work: The effects of diversity perspectives on work group processes and outcomes. *Administrative Science Quarterly, 46*(2), 229–273.

Engelmeier, S. (2018). *Inclusion: STILL the competitive business advantage*. eBookit.com.

Flory, T. (2015, September 1). Pornography has a big race problem. *Business Insider*. Retreived from https://www.businessinsider.com/pornography-has-a-big-race-problem-2015-9.

Galinsky, A. D., Todd, A. R., Homan, A. C., Phillips, K. W., Apfelbaum, E. P., Sasaki, S. J., … Maddux, W. W. (2015). Maximizing the gains and minimizing the pains of diversity: A policy perspective. *Perspectives on Psychological Science, 10*(6), 742–748. https://doi.org/10.1177/1745691615598513.

Hewlett, S. A., Rashid, R., & Sherbin, L. (2017). *Disrupt bias, drive value: A new path toward diverse, engaged, and fulfilled talent*. New York: Rare Bird Books.

Horne, M. S., Williamson, T. S., & Herman, A. (2018). *The contingent workforce: Business and legal strategies*. New York: Law Journal Press.

Joseph, R., & Selvaraj, P. (2015). The effects of work force diversity on employee performance in Singapore organisations. *International Journal of Business Administration, 6*(2), 17–29.

Klein, M. (2012). *America's war on sex: The continuing attack on law, lust, and liberty* (2nd ed.). Santa Barbara: ABC-CLIO.

Kopp, D. M., & Desiderio, K. P. (2009). Training's woeful countenance. *Human Resource Development Quarterly, 20*(1), 135–142.

Landes, X., & Nielsen, M. E. J. (2018). Racial dodging in the porn industry: A case with no silver bullet. *Porn Studies, 5*(2), 115–130. https://doi.org/10.1080/23268743.2018.1435302.

Loden, M., & Rosener, J. B. (1991). *Workforce America!: Managing employee diversity as a vital resource*. Homewood, IL: Business One Irwin.

Maitland, I. (2018). Why the business case for diversity is wrong. *Georgetown Journal of Law & Public Policy* (Special Issue), 731.

Markus, H. R., Steele, C. M., & Steele, D. M. (2000). Colorblindness as a barrier to inclusion: Assimilation and nonimmigrant minorities. *Daedalus, 129*(4), 233–259.

Mayall, A., & Russell, D. E. H. (1993). Racism in pornography. *Feminism & Psychology, 3*(2), 275–281. https://doi.org/10.1177/0959353593032023.

McMahon, A. M. (2010). Does workplace diversity matter? A survey of empirical studies on diversity and firm performance, 2000–09. *Journal of Diversity Management, 5*(2), 37–48.

Miller-Young, M. (2014). *A taste for brown sugar: Black women in pornography*. Durham, NC: Duke University Press.

Millward, J. (2013). *Deep inside: A study of 10,000 porn stars and their careers*. Retrieved from http://jonmillward.com/blog/studies/deep-inside-a-study-of-10000-porn-stars/.

Myers, V. (2013). *What if I say the wrong thing?: 25 habits for culturally effective people*. Chicago, IL: American Bar Association.

Page, S. E. (2008). *The difference: How the power of diversity creates better groups, firms, schools, and societies* (New ed.). Princeton, NJ: Princeton University Press.

Role, M. (2017). *Trans women in pornography: An exploration of the motivations and experiences of transgender women in the adult film industry.*

Santos, A. C., & Santos, A. L. (2018). Yes, we fuck! Challenging the misfit sexual body through disabled women's narratives. *Sexualities, 21*(3), 303–318. https://doi.org/10.1177/1363460716688680.

Segal, L. (1998). Only the literal: The contradictions of anti-pornography feminism. *Sexualities, 1*(1), 43–62. https://doi.org/10.1177/136346098001001003.

Senge, P. M. (2010). *The fifth discipline: The art and practice of the learning organization* (1st ed.). New York: Random House.

Shena, J., Ashok, C., D'Nettob, B., & Mongaa, M. (2009). Managing diversity through human resource management: An international perspective and conceptual framework. *International Journal of Human Resource Management, 20*(2), 235–251.

Shore, L. M., Randel, A. E., Chung, B. G., Dean, M. A., Holcombe Ehrhart, K., & Singh, G. (2011). Inclusion and diversity in work groups: A review

and model for future research. *Journal of Management, 37*(4), 1262–1289. https://doi.org/10.1177/0149206310385943.
Snow, A. (2018, June 23). The rise of racist porn. *Daily Beast*.
Soyka, P. A. (2012). *Creating a sustainable organization: Approaches for enhancing corporate value through sustainability*. Upper Saddle River, NJ: FT Press.
Tatli, A., & Ozbilgin, M. (2009). Understanding diversity managers' role in organizational change: Towards a conceptual framework. *Canadian Journal of Administrative Sciences, 26*(3), 244–258.
Thomas, D. A., & Ely, R. J. (1996, September–October). Making differences matter: A new paradigm for managing diversity. *Harvard Business Review, 74*(5), 79–90.
Turner, G. W., & Crane, B. (2016). Pleasure is paramount: Adults with intellectual disabilities discuss sensuality and intimacy. *Sexualities, 19*(5–6), 677–697. https://doi.org/10.1177/1363460715620573.
Walton, G., Murphy, M., & Ryan, A. M. (2105). Stereotype threat in organizations: Implications for equity and performance *The Annual Review of Organizational Psychology and Organizational Behavior, 2*(Annual), 523–550.
Wood, W. (1987). Meta analytical review of sex differences in group performance. *Psychological Bulletin, 102*(1), 53–71.
Young, J. H. (2005). Profound offense and cultural appropriation. *The Journal of Aesthetics and Art Criticism, 63*(2), 135–146.
Zhou, Y., & Paul, B. (2016). Lotus blossom or dragon lady: A content analysis of "Asian Women" online pornography. *Sexuality & Culture: An Interdisciplinary Quarterly, 20*, 1083–1100.

CHAPTER 6

Compensation and Benefits

Abstract In this chapter, the author explores the compensation framework in the pornography industry. Using recent data, the reader will get a sense as to the remuneration of different jobs within the industry. For example, a recent CNBC survey of pornography workers that the more extreme acts command higher rates, and the most extreme acts can go for $1800–$2500. Some performers intentionally wait on performing extreme or taboo acts as they develop their brand and fan base. The author also discusses passive income that adult performers receive, as well as access to healthcare is discussed.

Keywords Compensation · Passive income · Benefits · Insurance · Assembly Bill 5 · Independent contractor

Not surprisingly, many of the adult performers I interviewed were diffident regarding the specifics of how much they earned on the job. Having said that, the compensation framework in the pornography industry, I would find, is relatively straightforward.

Generally speaking, adult performers are paid as a function of the sex act needed for the video clip or scene. The rates for porn scenes vary based on the performer's gender and the kind of sex performed. "Scenes involving high-risk sex, such as anal cream-pies—internal ejaculate that is squeezed out—pay the most; those with no genital penetration generally

D. M. Kopp, *Human Resource Management in the Pornography Industry*, https://doi.org/10.1007/978-3-030-37659-8_6

Table 6.1 Pornography's adult performer compensation

Female performer, man/woman scene	\$900–\$1000
Female performer, all-woman scene	\$700–\$1200
Male performer	\$500–\$1000
Male/Girl Anal	\$1100–\$1200
Threesomes and Orgies	Base rate + \$200 per performer

Source Author's creation based on Morris (2016) and Snow (2016)

pay less" (Tarrant, 2016, p. 50). In fact, I learned from my field interviews that many adult performers intentionally wait on higher risk or taboo scenes until they are well-branded and can then create buzz within the fan base.

Like mainstream employees, sex workers, too, contemplate the compensation from a literal and abstract perspective; that is, the equity of the exchange of services. According to equity theory, there should be equity or the uniformity in the pay structure of a worker's remuneration. If the worker feels he or she is not being paid fairly for the amount of work he does in a day will result in lower productivity, increased turnover, and high absenteeism (Guest, 2017). This holds true in pornography's compensation world; for example, I interviewed an adult performer who stated that she would never agree to do a boy-girl scene for lower than \$800.

Using data from a recent CNBC survey[1] of pornography workers confirmed that the more extreme acts command higher rates (Table 6.1); the most extreme acts, not listed on the table, can range from \$1800 to \$12,000. The rates for the crew and staff behind the camera range from \$500 for a make-up artist to \$3000 for a director (Table 6.2).

As discussed prior, an adult performer's fan base and brand is tethered to potential sales. Those adult performers who have a large fan base and well-known brand can demand much higher pay (Miller, 2014). As described by former adult performer and director, Aurora Snow,

[1] https://www.cnbc.com/2016/01/20/porns-dirtiest-secret-what-everyone-gets-paid.html.

Table 6.2 Pornography's behind the camera compensation

Director	\$1000–\$3000
Cameraperson	\$500–\$700
Sound technician	\$300–\$400
Production assistant	\$100–\$250
Still photographers	\$500
Makeup artists	\$500

Source Author's creation based on Morris (2016) and Snow (2016)

> Mean Bitches CEO Glenn King doesn't balk at paying a performer more than his standard company rate if the math makes sense. It's a business equation. If I'm going to pay someone \$1200 instead of \$1000 then I need to be relatively confident that I'm going to make an extra \$200 off that scene, but the performer has to be popular. (Snow, 2016, https://fortune.com/2016/02/05/this-is-what-its-really-like-to-work-in-porn/)

Steve Hirsh, the owner of Vivid, one of the biggest adult entertainment studios, also explained,

> "When the girls first get into the business and they're new, I think they can command additional money for different sex acts. Initially they make more money, then it depends on how popular they become". (Morris, 2016, January 20, www.cnbc.com/2016/01/20/porns-dirtiest-secret-what-everyone-gets-paid.html)

And, today, it is through social media platforms such as Instagram, Facebook, YouTube, and Twitter that adult performers become part of that top-tier pool (Marwick, 2013; Miller, 2014). As of this writing, the most popular porn performers via their Instagram follower base were: Sunny Leone: 13.3 million followers, Mia Khalifa: 8.1 million followers, and Alexis Texas: 3.8 million followers.[2]

In addition to sex acts, many of the adult performers I interviewed were also expanding their revenue streams by diversifying beyond performing and were receiving passive income. For example, one female performer I interviewed rented out her own house for porn shoots and supplied wardrobe to other female performers.

[2] https://www.dailydot.com/irl/instagram-porn-stars/.

(Double) Penetration of the Glass-Ceiling with Barriers to Earning

Interestingly, whereas in other industries women, on average, make less than their male counterparts, there is a reverse gender wage gap in porn, at least as it relates to per scene sex acts. In 2012, a controversial Equal Pay Day PSA ran featuring porn star Sasha Grey telling women that if they want to earn as much as their male colleagues, they should do porn (Tibbals & Flynt, 2015)[3] For example, an unknown performer filming a girl-on-girl scene might make as little as $300, but if a popular star is involved in double penetration, she can rake in as much as $4000. Men earn between $500 and $1200 for the same scene (Snow, 2019).

I compensated some of my interviewees for their time. And, I was made aware that, for some, the PayPal or Venmo payment systems would have to be routed through a friend's account because there has been an issue with receiving funds through their adult website. In fact, in 2015, porn workers in the United States won two important legal rulings against financial institutions like Visa, JPMorgan, and PayPal who refuse to process payments from adult websites; some cases have seized earnings and closed bank accounts (Lee & Sullivan, 2016). As of this writing, PayPal ceased payouts to over 100,000 adult performers.

Another current compensation barrier issue affecting an adult performer's ability to earn a living surrounds the censorship of their social media accounts. APAG reported that as of March of 2019, 1374 individual performers had responded that their Instagram accounts (owned by Facebook) had been deactivated at one point. Still being negotiated as of this writing,[4] porn star Sybil Stallone told BuzzFeed News that she loses about $2000 every week that her account is deactivated because fans stop visiting her linked website, where she makes money from cam sessions and custom clips. "Like most sex workers I take care of my kids—my partner, my parents, and my disabled sibling," said Stallone via text. "That's the story; they are fucking with my money" (Steadman, 2019).[5]

[3] Gay male porn has a separate pay scale.

[4] Instagram policy team meets with APAG to listen to adult performers' concerns http://apagunion.com/2019/06/21/instagram-policy-team-meets-with-apag-listens-to-adult-performers-concerns/.

[5] The social media website Tumblr used to display adult content, but in November 2018, Apple removed Tumblr from its App Store after finding that child pornography

The Adult Performers Acting Guild (APAG) was moving forward against these companies for discrimination. "*APAG is currently working to organize those of you who have been affected, and work with the legal teams involved to seek justice and compensation*" (APAGunion.com).

As of this writing, APAG leaders, including their president Alana Evans, were having ongoing dialogue with the Instagram policy team, which included Public Policy executives at Facebook headquarters in the Bay Area. A transcript of their first meeting can be found on the APAG website,[6] which included this attention-grabbing exchange: "...Are nipples allowed?" asked APAG member Michelle Montana. "No," was said in unison by all the members of the Instagram team.

Both APAG and APAC advocate for the adult entertainment performer; below are the highlights of each organization (Table 6.3):

X-Rated Rosie the Riveters? Entrepreneurship = Empowerment[7]

Given the behemoth that is social media today with its various revenue streams available, more female performers in the adult industry are becoming entrepreneurs opting to create their own content, selling directly to fans through social media through feeds like OnlyFans.com, ManyVids, and Clips4Sale instead of turning to the male-dominated studios (Snow, 2019). As a result of this new female entrepreneurship in pornography, there is a neoteric dynamic and a new era regarding female adult performers vis-à-vis their compensation strategy and trajectory; new options are available whereby they no longer have to be on

had been found. A blanket ban was place on all adult content on December 17, 2018. The ban prohibited not just hardcore porn, but even the body parts such as the female nipple. As a result, Tumblr's web traffic dropped by about a third–both in the United States and internationally, according to analytics firm SimilarWeb from 558 million to 376 million monthly visits globally (Captain, 2019).

[6] http://apagunion.com/2019/06/21/instagram-policy-team-meets-with-apag-listens-to-adult-performers-concerns/.

[7] For millions of women *Rosie the Riveter* represented a launch to empowerment, both socially and economically in what had been up to that point a male-dominated labor world. Many believe that *Rosie the Riveter* heralded a new era for women's labor movement ushering in a critical change in social arrangements that would forever open up the work force to women (Kopp, 2007).

Table 6.3 Comparison between APAG and APAC

Name	Adult Performers Actors Guild	Adult Performer Advocacy Committee
Acronym	APAG	APAC
Website	http://apagunion.com/	https://www.apac-usa.com/
Tagline	United we bargain, divided we beg	Giving performers a voice both on set and off
Mission	To earn worker rights, set performers responsibilities, negotiate fair practices, and help performers provide themselves a better future	To advocate to maintain and improve safety and working conditions in the adult film industry with organized representation in matters that affect health, safety, and community
Member eligibility	Current or retired adult performer	Any person actively performing sexual acts on camera or other recorded representation produced or distributed for financial gain

Sources http://apagunion.com/; https://www.apac-usa.com/

a set every day. This shift within the pornography industry is consistent with the overarching trend in other industries of economic-based approach to female empowerment (McAdam, 2013; Tibbals & Flynt, 2015; Tooranian, 2018).

Adult Entertainers Employees vs. Independent Contractors

As discussed prior, perhaps the biggest financial impact affecting adult performers—this change actually transpiring while I was writing this book—is that many of them would now be considered employees eligible for overtime pay versus the independent contractors of the gig economy.

California governor Gavin Newsom signed Assembly Bill 5, the state's rewritten employment law, much of the focus was on Uber and Lyft drivers. Under the law, performers in the adult entertainment industry are entitled to the same benefits as those drivers, specifically being recognized as employees of the companies they work for. That gives them the right to overtime pay, minimum wage protection, and workers' compensation protections (Morris, 2019).

In September 2019, the California Labor Federation put out this statement via Twitter, "As a worker in the adult industry, the moment you walk on to set, your employer is responsible for your safety. Being recognized as an employee will ensure you are protected, paid properly & more prepared for your future"[8]

Dr. Chauntelle Tibbals, a sociologist who specializes in the world of adult entertainment, confirmed,

> For performers, it's probably not going to have much of a negative impact, aside from the fact that they'll see less money...They're used to getting their day rate. Now they're going to have taxes taken out of it. It is also going to cost producers time and money to do that. (as cited by Morris, 2019)

However, because few porn stars work 40-hour weeks, being provided healthcare is still not likely.

Porn Stars and Deductibles

At the adult industry trade shows I attended, I would often attempt to "break the ice" with a prospective adult performer interviewee; this was a typical exchange (and response):

> *Author*: Hello, can I ask you a question you've probably never been asked before?
> *Adult Performer*: I doubt that, hon. Go ahead.
> *Author*: Okay, great...do you have medical and dental insurance?
> *Adult Performer*: (bemused)...

Unlike with performers, the retail, non-performer side of the pornography is well-insured. The larger pornography companies, for the most part, have employer-sponsored benefits, worker's compensation, and the full suite of coverages you would expect from a traditional business. Yet, as I would learn from interviews with performers and insurance brokers who service the adult entertainment industry, many adult performers are, in fact, like many conventional workers, either self-insured or on Medicaid (especially if they had children).[9] Still, there are organizations that assist

[8] https://twitter.com/CaliforniaLabor.

[9] The Census found that 8.5% of the US population went without medical insurance for all of 2018, up from 7.9% in 2017.

those workers in pornography who would seek health and life insurance. Examples of this are the Free Speech Coalition (FSC), a trade association for the adult entertainment industry, as well as APAG who also partners with insurance brokers to provide access to health benefits and life insurance to those who worked in pornography. A sample of the offerings was found on their respective websites:

> *We have established a relationship with an A + rated life insurance company to provide up to $249,999 of death benefit to our members and their families without a medical exam with the option to purchase higher death benefits with underwriting. This is part of an ongoing campaign by the Free Speech Coalition to provide access to an array of benefits with adult-aware partners.* (https://www.freespeechcoalition.com/programs/health-insurance/)

> *Since most companies treat adult performers as freelance contractors, employer health insurance is nearly nonexistent. While we work to fix this issue in our industry, help is still available to get you and your family covered! As open enrollment approaches, this is the time for you to start planning and get prepared. The Adult Performers Actors Guild can help you in the process. We have experts who can help you get insurance with a premium that fits within your budget. Our experts are available to members at no cost! They will personally help you through the entire enrollment process to get you and your dependents insured.* (http://apagunion.com/performer-info/health-insurance/)

Importantly, and as discussed further in the next chapter, access to mental health resources, especially, is a highlighted need in today's porn industry.

References

Captain, S. (2019). After Tumblr's NSFW ban, these adult communities have come out on top. *Fast Company*.

Guest, D. (2017). Human resource management and employee well-being: Towards a new analytic framework: HRM and employee well-being: New analytic framework. *Human Resource Management Journal, 27*, 22–38. https://doi.org/10.1111/1748-8583.12139.

Kopp, D. M. (2007). Rosie the riveter: A training perspective. *Human Resource Development Quarterly, 18*(4), 589–597.
Lee, J., & Sullivan, R. (2016). Porn and labour: The labour of porn studies. *Porn Studies, 3*(2), 104–106. London: Taylor & Francis.
Marwick, A. E. (2013). *Status update: Celebrity, publicity, and branding in the social media age*. Haven, CT: Yale University Press.
McAdam, M. (2013). *Female entrepreneurship*. London: Routledge.
Miller, A. (2014). Confessions of a pornographer! Interview with Kevin Moore. *Something Awful*. Retrieved from https://www.somethingawful.com/comedy-goldmine/kevin-moore-porn/5/.
Morris, C. (Producer). (2016). Porn's dirtiest secret: What everyone gets paid. *CNBC*. Retrieved from https://www.cnbc.com/2016/01/20/porns-dirtiest-secret-what-everyone-gets-paid.html.
Morris, C. (2019). Adult entertainers are now eligible for overtime pay. *Fortune*.
Snow, A. (2016, February 5). This is what it's really like to work in porn. *Fortune*.
Snow, A. (2019, May 11). How porn's women are taking their power back: 'I'm in control'. *Daily Beast*.
Steadman, O. (2019). *Porn stars vs. Instagram: Inside the battle to remain on the platform*.
Tarrant, S. (2016). *The pornography industry: What everyone needs to know*. New York: Oxford University Press.
Tibbals, C., & Flynt, T. (2015). *Exposure: A sociologist explores sex, society, and adult entertainment*. Austin, TX: Greenleaf Book Group Press.
Tooranian, F. (2018). *Empowerment: A hegemonic approach for women in informal settlements*. University of Auckland.

CHAPTER 7

Workplace Health and Safety

Abstract In this chapter, the author explores the health and safety practices in the pornography industry. Adult film industry workers face serious health risks due to potential infection with HIV and other pathogens transmitted through sexual contact. The author will look into recent legislation impacting the pornography industry such as Proposition 60 in California which enforces the existing mandatory condom rule and provide other health protections for adult film performers. Also, OSHA and workers compensation is discussed.

Keywords OSHA · PASS database · FLOW · Proposition 60 · Workers compensation · Mental health

Workplace health and safety are main foci in HRM practice from both a legal compliance and the strategic approach to HRM (Danna & Griffin, 1999; Guest, 2017). Generally, the two domains of workplace health and safety center on both the physical and the psychosocial work environment and each contributes to the overarching construct of *well-being* (Danna & Griffin, 1999; Dollard, Dormann, & Idris, 2019; van Veldhoven & Peccei, 2014). Within the concept of well-being lie the dimensions of *objective* and *subjective* well-being. Objective well-being is tethered to such variables as health, economics, and physical work environment; subjective well-being includes a worker's considerations of his or her

D. M. Kopp, *Human Resource Management in the Pornography Industry*, https://doi.org/10.1007/978-3-030-37659-8_7

meaningfulness, sense of purpose, and value of his or her life—the so-called "hedonic and eudaimonic aspects of quality of work life" (Schulte et al., 2015, p. 66).

On the Objective Well-Being of Sex Workers

Camera-facing performers in pornography encounter serious health risks due to the potential of sexually transmitted infections and other pathogens transferred through sexual contact (Grudzen, Ryan, Margold, Torres, & Gelberg, 2009).

Underscoring this risk even further is that the workers in pornography are classified as "gig workers"—that is, they are independent contractors, not employees. Consequently, the Occupational Safety and Health Administration (OSHA)—the federal agency created to protect employees from health and safety hazards on the job[1]—currently has no jurisdiction in the adult entertainment industry.[2] Organizations who use independent contractors only have a duty to take "reasonable care" to avoid an unsafe workplace versus the higher duty required to provide a safe work environment for their employees (Cohen & Eimicke, 2013; Fishman, 2003), including training and supervising them.

There have been, however, recent efforts by gig workers to challenge their independent contractor status. These entreaties have been buoyed by the changing nature of work and the continuing expansion of contingent employment contracts. According to Connelly and Gallagher (2006) there is, in fact, a distinction between what can be labeled as "independent contracting" arrangements, where the workers are autonomous and mobile, and other situations where workers are more *dependent* on their clients, so-called "dependent contractors" (p. 12)—such seems to be the case of the adult performer.

[1] And, the respective state level counterpart.

[2] OSHA's oversight appears valuable given recent data from the US Bureau of Labor Statistics compiled in an AFL-CIO report show an increase in work-related fatalities involving independent contractors (Trumka, Shuler, & Gebre, 2017).

Lawsuits first filed by Uber drivers brought into question if some gig workers were being misclassified as contractors when they really should have been considered employees.[3]

The Adult Performers Actors Guild (APAG) recently advocated for new legislation in California for Assembly Bill (AB) 5.[4] The bill passed in September 2019, and it further regulates the gig economy by mandating many gig companies to reclassify their independent contractors as employees with the attendant benefits therein, and this would include sex workers (Griswold, 2019). The Bill is particularly impactful because workers in pornography were not only ineligible for workers' compensation coverage—were they to be injured on the job—but also sex workers have limited legal protection should they complain about said working conditions (Craver et al., 2019). The effect is that the pornography worker is no longer self-regulated and self-insured vis-à-vis workplace health and safety[5] in what is unquestionably a physically and emotionally challenging trade. Consider the following rich descriptions of a day in the life of adult performers by porn veteran Aurora Snow and producer and sex worker Andre Shakti:

> An adult film set is a uniquely employed workplace. Here, employees are required to be nude. It calls for full physical contact among coworkers that, at times, may call for choking, slapping, hitting, maybe hair pulling, and intrusive bodily acts. It can be messy, degrading, or empowering work, which makes this particular work environment especially difficult to navigate. (Snow, 2016)
>
> In my relatively short career, I've received genital burn from hours of condom friction, been hit in the head with a large vibrator when one was tossed to me, slipped on multiple sneaky patches of spilled silicone lube, and actually torn my rotator cuff during a pornographic wrestling match.

[3] In April 2019, drivers for Uber were deemed independent contractors and not employees; the general counsel of a US labor agency concluded in an advisory memo to the National Labor Relations Board (NLRB).

[4] http://apagunion.com/2019/09/30/ab5-5-passes-in-california-making-many-independent-contractors-employees/.

[5] Regulatory agencies have been slow to adapt to the gig economy. Interest groups like the National Council for Occupational Safety and Health have lobbied OSHA to enforce workplace safety issues in the gig economy under a "dual employer" theory. This would make the gig company responsible for safety compliance, even though the gig worker is not an employee of the hiring organization (Shaw, 2019).

> This doesn't include the numerous mornings I've woken up, after a shoot, feeling like I was hit with a truck. Too many upside-down pile-drivers; not enough stretching. Please repeat after me: Porn is for consumption, not imitation! (Shakti, 2015)

Grudzen et al. (2009) detailed the risks of physical trauma within the pornography listing such events as:

- Chemical burns from sex toys
- Wounds due to penile injections
- Anal tears
- Cuts and bruises
- Being slapped, having hair pulled on set by other performers
- Asphyxiation
- Simulating rape or violence in the scene

It is worth noting that in addition to legislative efforts, there are activists within and formerly in the pornography industry who have endeavored to improve the health and safety conditions in the pornography industry. Advocates include former adult performers who campaign by way of their cautionary tales. Such is the case with Cameron Adams, a former porn performer who was known in the industry as "Cameron Bay." Adams was only in porn for a few months in 2013, but during that time she sustained a serious injury to her breast, got a serious kidney infection, and contracted HIV (Miles, 2014).[6]

Advocacy groups like *Sexworkers Project* (http://sexworkersproject.org/), as well as porn companies, have memorialized their efforts to keep the physical work environment safe. KINK.com, for example, lists on their website the health and safety guidelines for their models[7] (excerpted below):

[6] It is worth noting that web sites like antipornography.org, findthenewdrug.org, and collectiveshout.org detail injuries and safety concerns within the pornography industry from an anti-(s)exploitation and dangers of pornography lens.

[7] https://www.kink.com/model-rights.

Health and Safety

- I am entitled to ask for and use a condom at any time, for any reason. If I do choose to use a condom, it will in no way affect my ability to book future scenes for Kink.
- I am entitled to ask to see fresh condoms applied to any item used on me.
- I am entitled to personally sanitize any items that are used on me.
- I am entitled to ask anyone touching my genitals to wear sanitary gloves.
- I am entitled to ask to have any item tested on me before the scene begins (examples: nipple clamps, gags, etc.).

Safewords

- I can stop any scene at any time by using the house safeword "RED" or the safeword I chose before filming began.
- I will have a recognizable nonverbal safeword signal in the event that I am gagged or otherwise unable to speak. (examples: looking directly at the camera, foot stomping, dropping an item held in the hand)
- Upon use of my safeword, the scene will stop, but cameras will remain rolling for my safety. I am entitled to ask for the shoot to completely end. Only if I explicitly consent can the scene continue at a slower pace.

Safety Initiatives in the Pornography Industry

Interestingly, support for safety initiatives has been mixed within the pornography industry. For example, Measure B, also known as the County of Los Angeles *Safer Sex in the Adult Film Industry Act*, is the law that requires the use of condoms in all vaginal and anal sex scenes in pornography productions filmed in Los Angeles County, California. The measure also requires porn production companies to obtain a health permit prior to production and to post the permit and a notice to performers regarding condom use during production (Grudzen et al., 2009).

While Measure B passed, there were some in the industry who did not support the measure. In February 2016, Prop 60 Cal-OSHA, the

Los Angeles County's workplace safety and health regulatory agency that oversees the porn industry, narrowly rejected condom rules for performers that were advocated by the San Francisco-based AIDS Healthcare Foundation. Not one active porn performer spoke in favor of the proposed regulations (Beard, 2017; Bindel, 2018; Lee & Sullivan, 2016; Tarrant, 2016).

Presently, the standard protocol for adult talent involves voluntary testing done every fourteen days. Once tests are completed, the results are entered into the Performer Availability Screening Services (PASS), a database that is maintained by the Free Speech Coalition, a trade association for the adult entertainment industry. Prior to a shoot, producers, directors, and the talent departments check the PASS database; the PASS data is also available to performers on request (https://fscpass.com/).[8]

Given these current safety protocols and practices within the pornography industry, adult performer, Alix Lovell, shared with me that she genuinely believed that the porn industry saved her life. Prior to joining the industry, she was having frequent sex, but in a less safe manner; she went on to reflect, "You know, going into porn probably saved my life." (Personal Interview, February, 2019)

Porn Workers in FLOW?

Given the backdrop of work that is difficult and very demanding, both physically and emotionally, as discussed, access to mental health resources seems to be particularly vital in today's pornography industry. Nevertheless, what consistently emerged from my interviews with adult performers was how vocal they were in their confidence of their skill set and abilities[9] in their work. Quotes like, "I am very good at sex" and "I have special skills (wink)" were not uncommon in my field interviews. To be sure, adult performers being talented at sex should come to no one's surprise. In his book, *Outliers*, (Gladwell, 2008), Canadian author and

[8] In April, 2017, APAC called for an Immediate Production Hold due to an adult industry performer testing positive for HIV. The Adult Performer Advocacy Committee (APAC) requested a temporary industry-wide production hold while doctors perform confirmatory tests. Based on the current genealogy, it was determined that there was low-risk to the performer pool, but APAC released a statement within the following days regarding a two-week moratorium.

[9] Such aplomb within the industry was memorialized in books like, *The Porn Star Guide to Great Sex* (Marcus, 2010).

journalist Malcolm Gladwell introduced his 10,000-Hour Rule, which he considers the key to success in any field. Here, practicing something for 10,000 hours can give rise to personal mastery. I will let the reader do the math vis-à-vis adult performers.

Having such emerged themes of high *challenge* of the extreme working conditions and a high *skill set*, led me to consider the concept of FLOW.

Hungarian psychologist Mihaly Csikszentmihalyi first described the construct of *flow* as a completely focused motivation, a single-minded immersion that represents the ultimate engagement while in the service of performing (Csikszentmihalyi, 1990). Specifically, from a knowledge, skills, and attitudes (KSAs) standpoint, one might frame resolute job engagement as follows:

- Head—"I am mentally engaged in the work"
- Hands—"I am engaged in doing the work"
- Heart—I am emotionally engaged in the work".[10]

Other researchers similarly have defined work engagement with the dimensions of vigor, dedication, and absorption[11] (Amabile & Kramer, 2013; Bates & Davis, 2010; Schaufeli, Salanova, González-Romá, & Bakker, 2002). Not surprisingly, and irrespective of industry, a worker's motivation on the job plays a significant part in the job performance; that is, as a worker's on-the-job motivation goes, so goes his or her job performance.

Particularly, in the flow model,[12] the state of a worker's motivation is based on the status and interaction of two forces: the worker's skills set, or ability (high or low), and the worker's assessment of the challenges of the job (high or low); as a result, a state of flow can be realized when, within the context of performance, the *work's high challenge meets the worker's high skill* (Table 7.1).[13]

[10] Corporate Leadership Council, Best Practices to Engage Employees, 2009

[11] The Utrecht Work Engagement Scale (UWES) measures such dimensions

[12] The author is utilizing the 4-channel version of FLOW

[13] Anxiety can be both positive and negative; usually anxiety becomes negative when it is chronic vs. episodic

Table 7.1 Domains of FLOW

Domain	*Employee skill set*	*Workplace challenge*	*Resulting motivation*
Apathy	LOW	LOW	Negative
Boredom	HIGH	LOW	Negative
Anxiety	LOW	HIGH	Positive/negative
Flow	HIGH	HIGH	Positive

Source Adapted from Csikszentmihalyi (1990)

On Sex Workers Subjective Well-Being

Between November 2017 and January 2018, at least five adult performers died due to alleged drug overdoses or by suicide. In the aftermath, the pornography industry reacted to the unprecedented trend with a call-to-action for more mental health resources within the adult entertainment industry, including creating their own support groups for sex workers (Monk-Turner & Turner, 2010; Severin, 2018). APAC also released a statement, which read, in part:

> At APAC, we see that our community faces the stigma that comes with being in adult film. Compounding that with the stigma surrounding mental health issues and the pursuit of mental health support, we see the intersectional challenges that our community faces. A continued aim at APAC is to combat the stigma through which the world views sex work as well as the internal stigma within our own industry. (https://www.apac-usa.com/)

In addition to literal physical safety, safety and security needs include emotional security, as well. Ashforth and Kreiner (1999) proposed that morally stigmatized dirty workers are more likely—than members of physically or socially tainted occupations—to rely on the collective or other occupational members as sources of social validation.

Today, in the pornography industry, mental health services are more accessible than ever before; it is not uncommon to see APAC and other adult performer support groups host mental health forums for the adult film industry.

References

Amabile, T., & Kramer, S. (2013). *The progress principle: Using small wins to ignite joy, engagement, and creativity at work*. Boston, MA: Perseus Books Group.

Ashforth, B., & Kreiner, G. (1999). How can you do it?: Dirty work and the challenge of constructing a positive identity. *The Academy of Management Review, 24*(3), 413–434.

Bates, D., & Davis, T. (2010). The application bridge: A model for improving trainee engagement in the training process. *International Journal of Management, 27*(3), 770–777.

Beard, M. (2017). Porn with purpose: why retrofitting social responsibility never works in business. *The Guardian*.

Bindel, J. (2018). The truth about the porn industry. *The Guardian*. Retrieved from https://www.theguardian.com/lifeandstyle/2010/jul/02/gail-dines-pornography.

Cohen, S., & Eimicke, W. (2013). *Independent Contracting: Policy and Management Analysis*. Retrieved from New York.

Connelly, C. E., & Gallagher, D. G. (2006). Independent and dependent contracting: Meaning and implications. *Human Resource Management Review, 16*(2), 95–106. https://doi.org/10.1016/j.hrmr.2006.03.008.

Craver, C. B., Rothstein, M. A., Hébert, L. C., Lobel, O., Malloy, S. E., McCormick, M., … Shoben, E. W. (2019). *Employment Law*. West Academic.

Csikszentmihalyi, M. (1990). *Flow: The psychology of optimal experience*. New York: Harper & Row.

Danna, K., & Griffin, R. W. (1999). Health and well-being in the workplace: A review and synthesis of the literature. *Journal of Management, 25*(3), 357–384. https://doi.org/10.1016/S0149-2063(99)00006-9.

Dollard, M. F., Dormann, C., & Idris, M. A. (2019). *Psychosocial safety climate: A New Work stress theory*. Cham: Springer International Publishing.

Fishman, S. (2003). *Hiring Independent Contractors: The Employers' Legal Guide*. Berkeley, CA: Nolo.

Gladwell, M. (2008). *Outliers: The story of success*. New York: Little, Brown.

Griswold, A. (2019). The gig is up: California is about to rewrite the rules of the gig economy. *Quartz*. Retrieved from https://qz.com/1703897/californias-ab5-will-rewrite-the-rules-of-the-gig-economy/.

Grudzen, C. R., Ryan, G., Margold, W., Torres, J., & Gelberg, L. (2009). Pathways to health risk exposure in adult film performers. *Journal of Urban Health: Bulletin of the New York Academy of Medicine, 86*(1), 67–78. https://doi.org/10.1007/s11524-008-9309-4.

Guest, D. (2017). Human resource management and employee well-being: Towards a new analytic framework: HRM and employee well-being: New analytic framework. *Human Resource Management Journal, 27*, 22–38. https://doi.org/10.1111/1748-8583.12139.

Lee, J., & Sullivan, R. (2016). Porn and labour: The labour of porn studies. *Porn Studies, 3*(2), 104–106. London: Taylor & Francis.

Marcus, M. (2010). *The porn star guide to great sex*. New York: St. Martin's Publishing Group.

Miles, K. (2014). *Cameron Bay, porn performer with HIV, Recalls disturbing experiences on set, where condoms weren't used*. Retrieved from https://www.huffpost.com/entry/cameron-bay-porn-hiv_n_3867014.

Monk-Turner, E., & Turner, C. (2010). Subjective well-being among those who exchange sex and money, Yunnan, China and Thailand. *Social Indicators Research, 99*(1), 13–23.

Schaufeli, W. B., Salanova, M., González-Romá, V., & Bakker, A. B. (2002). The measurement of engagement and burnout: A confirmative analytic approach. *Journal of Happiness Studies, 3*, 71–92.

Schulte, P. A., Guerin, R. J., Schill, A. L., Bhattacharya, A., Cunningham, T. R., Pandalai, S. P., ... Stephenson, C. M. (2015). Considerations for incorporating "well-being" in public policy for workers and workplaces. *American Journal of Public Health, 105*(8), e31–e44. https://doi.org/10.2105/AJPH.2015.302616.

Severin, K. (2018). Mental illness is killing porn stars and the industry is taking action. *VICE*.

Shakti, A. (2015). 9 Hilariously unsexy things you never knew about porn: As told by a porn actress. *Cosmopolitan*.

Shaw, S. (2019). *Workplace safety in the gig economy: New hazards and liabilities*.

Snow, A. (2016, 2/5/2016). This is what it's really like to work in porn. *Fortune*.

Tarrant, S. (2016). *The pornography industry: What everyone needs to know*. New York: Oxford University Press.

Trumka, R., Shuler, E., & Gebre, T. (2017). *Death on the job: The toll of neglect*. Retrieved from Washington, DC: 2019.

van Veldhoven, M., & Peccei, R. (2014). *Well-being and performance at work: The role of context*. Abingdon: Taylor & Francis.

CHAPTER 8

Porn and HRM: Axiological Issues

Abstract The concluding chapter explores the overarching questions that are presented in the introductory chapter as well as lessons learned. One benefit of examining aspects of HR in situ within the context of a so-called pariah industry is that we are better positioned to reflect upon another theme proffered here, specifically, one that considers the axiology of human resources: is HR amoral? In other words, the construct of HR, like with food, water, and oxygen is—*prima facie*—value-neutral; that is, until seemingly placed into a context where it risks being rendered guilty by association. In sum, we contemplate the question, Does "dirty work" equate to "dirty HR"?

Keywords Axiology · Future research · Corporate social responsibility · Values · Sin industries

"*Postremo postcoital*"

Having explored the operational nuances and practical aspects of HRM in the pornography industry, overarching themes, and lessons learned, questions that may still remain unanswered can now be contemplated and positioned well for future researchers. And, while still honoring my

D. M. Kopp, *Human Resource Management in the Pornography Industry*, https://doi.org/10.1007/978-3-030-37659-8_8

initial pledge to avoid "Kantian debates regarding the morality of pornography," it does not preclude us from reflecting sagaciously on the axiology of HRM in the context of the pornography industry.

Dirty Work Equals Dirty HRM?

Do "sin industries" have sinful HRM? What emerged for me—phenomenologically—was that *the taint of "dirty work" seemed to extend to the processes that support said dirty work*; that is, HRM in a stigmatized trade tends to stigmatize that HRM. And, while some may argue that there are ethical responsibilities in the practice of HRM that are irrespective of industry (e.g., Klikauer, 2014), I gleaned a 'guilt-by-association' vis-à-vis HRM and the pornography industry.[1] In sum, the construct of HRM, like with food, water, and oxygen, is—prima facie—value neutral until placed into a context.[2] The organization (and its HRM) transmute to an *organization-as-pariah*.

As previously discussed, my fieldwork in pornography was subjected to regular questioning about the social and academic value from peers, students, and close friends. This premise is validated when, for example, an unsympathetic public may victim blame a sex worker who is exploited or demoralized on the job—disdain is also extended to the porn company that hired her; this is consistent with Kulik's et al. findings that there is a "stigma by association" (Kulik, Bainbridge, & Cregan, 2008). Contrast that dynamic to those who may be genuinely nonplussed to hear anything untoward occurring at Disney, Southwest Airlines, or Amazon.[3]

As a researcher, evaluating a construct's mutable axiology was not unfamiliar to me. During my study of the social history of training (Kopp, 2018), I realized that training systems were, in practice, the means to facilitate the ends of what might be stratified as the good, the bad, and the

[1] To be sure, this would be the position of Gail Dines, professor emerita of sociology and women's studies at Wheelock College in Boston and the founder of an anti-pornography group called *Culture Reframed*. Dines rejects anything related to pornography as ethical. She has said that something that exploits and commodifies and monetizes women's bodies is not ethical, and this would presumably include anything (e.g., HRM) that facilitates that, as well.

[2] I also made this point regarding the social history of training, as well (Kopp, 2018).

[3] These companies consistently rank as having top human resource departments https://www.workforce.com/2019/04/25/2019-workforce-100-ranking-top-companies-hr/.

dubious of society. So, for example, the value neutral training propositions of "properly utilizing an individual's unused capabilities," and "using small ratios of trainees to trainers" seamlessly transmogrify to *bad* training after we learn that these are excerpted from the al Qaeda training manual (U.S. Department of Justice, 2000, pp. 15, 47). And, in the same way, we may consider the *good* training used by the not-for-profit *Dress for Success* organization that empowers women by training them on life skills such as interviewing techniques and résumé writing so as to promote economic independence and self-sufficiency (*Dress for Success*, 2006).

In sum, the assertion I proffered was that while training itself may be value neutral, training programs have historically been the means to sustain stereotypes, racism, anti-Semitism, and prejudice, in general. Whether as part of sexist ephemera (think: *airline hostess* training) or fanatical cultural movements (think: the Hitler Youth training manual) training—especially vocational training has borne witness to and/or aided and abetted human events, in both triumph and disgrace.

Thus, like the construct of training, by anthropomorphizing HRM, too, and then tethering it to consequentialist and non-consequentialist ethical considerations, we can more effectively reflect on HRM's virtue within any social context. This tests Waytz's, Epley's, and Cacioppo's (2010) assertion that when something is anthropomorphized, it renders it worthy of moral consideration.

Such contemplations fall under the critical perspective of HRM (Armstrong, 1999; Bolton, 2010; Cai, Jo, & Pan, 2012); specifically, critical HRM including reflecting on the impacts of HRM practice not only to organizations and individuals, but to society, at large. This sets us up well for a brief discussion on corporate social responsibility (CSR).

Dirty Work, Dirty HRM, and Dirty CSR

Critical HRM challenges the status quo and the one-dimensional nature of HRM. Critical HRM is responsive to context, power and inequality (Alvesson, 2009); this is of value to the field because, heretofore, HRM research has remained passive in asking questions related to the epistemological and ontological issues (Itani, 2017). Importantly, critical HRM focuses less on the "*what*" and "*how*" of HRM, but shifts the emphasis toward the "*why*" of HRM with the everyday processes and human actions that occur in the workplace and their impact on workers and the

Table 8.1 Should organizations be in the CSR business?

For	*Against*
The rise of the modern corporation created and continues to create many social problems. Therefore, the corporate world should assume responsibility for addressing these problems	Taking on social and moral issues is not economically feasible. Corporations should focus on earning a profit for their shareholders and leave social issues to others
In the long run, it is in corporations' best interest to assume social responsibilities. It will increase the chances that they will have a future and reduce the chances of increased governmental regulation	Assuming social responsibilities places those corporations doing so at a competitive disadvantage relative to those who do not
Large corporations have huge reserves of human and financial capital. They should devote at least some of their resources to addressing social issues	Those who are most capable should address social issues. Those in the corporate world are not equipped to deal with social problems

Source Adapted from http://www.referenceforbusiness.com/management/Comp-De/Corporate-Social-Responsibility.html#ixzz2LSk4PPE7

local community in which any work organization is situated (Armstrong, 1999; Bolton, 2010; Bratton & Gold, 2015).

An extension of critical HRM is the concept of corporate social responsibility (CSR); CSR is a commitment by organizations "to behave ethically and contribute to economic development while improving the quality of life of the workforce and their families as well as the local community and society at large" (Watts, 1999, p. 3; see also: Cai et al., 2012; Frederick, 1998; Gond, Igalens, Swaen, & Akremi, 2011).

In fact, there is debate as to whether any organization should be in the CSR space at all (see Table 8.1); while some agree with the benefits of CSR for organizations, others question the nature of CSR and argue that it is in conflict with business profitability. Perhaps not surprisingly, the pornography industry's initiatives, particularly, in CSR have been blunted.[4] Specifically, attempts by the porn industry to donate to charities is looked askance (Beard, 2017); and, while donations are accepted

[4] For Arbor Day in 2014, Pornhub came up with "Gives America Wood" and planted a tree for a certain number of hits for one "related" video category. Pornhub sponsored the planting of over 15,000 trees, but to the embarrassment of the donee charity (Altman, 2014).

from the pornography industry, the interaction is treated in a way that appears shame-based and furtive (Altman, 2014).

For example, in 2017, Pornhub™, the world's biggest porn site, launched a sex education platform known as the sexual wellness center[5]. As described by Pornhub, the sexual wellness center is "an online resource aiming to provide readers with information and advice regarding sexuality, sexual health and relationships." Fessler (2017) pointed out that the irony of Pornhub's endeavor—saying that if any industry has negatively impacted young peoples' understanding of healthy sexual behavior, it is mainstream porn. *Girls and Sex* (Orenstein, 2017) author Peggy Ornstein, too, critiqued Pornhub's CSR efforts,

> Ultimately, Pornhub is entering territory it—by warrant of its affiliations—may best avoid. Sexual education is really not their purpose. it's...a white-washing scam to justify the kind of anti-female pleasure, misogynist, distorted sexuality that often eroticizes humiliation, that's devoid of intimacy, and at best mis-represents female pleasure. Creating a sexual wellness site, says Ornstein, seems like a way to get away with the abusive mainstream pornography Pornhub otherwise promotes. (Fessler, 2017, https://qz.com/902750/pornhub-the-worlds-biggest-purveyor-of-online-porn-wants-to-teach-its-users-where-babies-come-from/)

Yet, Pornhub's Vice President Corey Price was positive that efforts to disassociate charity from porn were waning:

> People are slowly becoming more open minded about being associated with us," he states. We try to conduct ourselves in a way that steers clear of fulfilling people's preconceived notions of vulgarity, in preference of class and tastefulness. (as quoted by Altman, 2014)

Doing Well While Doing Bad?

Notwithstanding, research still supports the benefits of an organization's CSR initiatives, even in so-called sin industries; further, (and importantly) leaders in sin industries see the value of CSR even when their products are considered harmful to people, society, or the environment (Cai et al., 2012). Consider, independent of the product—whether porn, orange

[5] https://www.pornhub.com/sex/.

juice or diapers—ethical egoism (and capitalism) would still dictate that organizations act to create the greatest benefits they can for themselves and make decisions to achieve the organizational goal of maximizing profits (Österberg, 2012).

Adult website *Benevidz* founder Mike Wondercub explains how Benevidz gathers 10–20% of its performers' gratuities into one pot and then each month they elect a different charity. The donations are discreetly donated to chosen cause. "You have to build a relationship with the charities. The stigma is real, but we don't run into it as much because we're low-key. "Charity as part of the porn's business model" (Smith, 2014).

Wondercub's view tethers us to the initial themes presented early on in the book; that is, sexually explicit material becoming pornography when it is produced for and part of a profit-seeking business model—Rose's (2013) pornography-capitalism link. To be sure, as a contrast, there is a dearth of CSR with the obfuscated status of pornography within dictatorships (Cowan, 2016).

Cum Hither: Human Resource Management in the Pornography Industry

In exploring HRM within the pornography industry we reaffirm that this industry faces much of the same operational considerations as typical, for-profit industries, including social responsibility expectations. Moreover, a collateral intention to this book was to destigmatize pornography a reaction to the outgrowth of what sociologist Jan Kalenda sees as a sociocultural change in current lifestyle as part of late modernity or what Bauman (2013) called *liquid* modernity, as Kalenda (2016) writes, owing to late modernity,

> ...when it came to its legalization, legitimization and interconnection with the economic sector...it [pornography] has ceased to be seen only in negative connotations and has begun to be seen in a new way, as one of the many ambivalent, late modern features of social reality. (p. 68)

Such sociocultural assessments are not trivial as they not only influence HR practice, but also may dictate how the discipline of human resources itself labels, regards, and accepts other so-called stigmatized "dirty work" and, specifically, other *dirty workers* who may be independently contracted.

In addition, the pornography industry's use of independent workers can offer lessons learned as the field of human resources interacts with other industries that subcontract out their workers, as well. Indeed, the field of HR may need to adjust its practice; in HRM today there are growing models that move away from the traditional employer-employee relationship. A notable example is seen in the rise of employee leasing, where employees are leased and the company pays a fee to the leasing firm or the consultancy that handles employee benefits, payroll, and all other HR functions on behalf of the client company. Outsourcing, too, where companies outsource or assign the task of recruitment to the third-party specialist, who then carry out all the recruitment activities which would have been done in-house otherwise (Werner & DeSimone, 2011). Yet, we can conclude that there still is a need for HR management at a workplace with self-employed contractors.

In the final analysis, exploring HRM practices in the pornography may be justified if only because, like Mountaineer George Mallory's response as to why he wanted to climb Mt. Everest—"Because it's there," but more worthy it follows that, inter alia, examining the pornography industry in the context of human resource management presents an opportunity to utilize the sociocultural changes in business studies for a more inclusive setting regarding business practices in all domains of business—including those industries in the shadows due to stigmatized trades.

References

Altman, L. (2014). Charities Hush about porn industry donations. *Non Profit Quaterly*.

Alvesson, M. (2009). *Critical perspectives on strategic HRM*. London: Routledge.

Armstrong, M. (1999). *A handbook of human resource management practice* London: UK: Kogan Page.

Bauman, Z. (2013). *Liquid modernity*. Oxford: Wiley.

Beard, M. (2017). Porn with purpose: Why retrofitting social responsibility never works in business. *The Guardian*.

Bolton, S. (2010). *Critical human resource management*. New York: Sage.

Bratton, J., & Gold, J. (2015). Towards Critical Human Resource Management Education (CHRME): A sociological imagination approach. *Work, Employment & Society, 29*(3), 496–507. https://doi.org/10.1177/0950017014545266.

Cai, Y., Jo, H., & Pan, C. (2012). Doing well while doing bad? CSR in controversial industry sectors. *Journal of Business Ethics, 108*. https://doi.org/10.1007/s10551-011-1103-7.

Cowan, B. A. (2016). *Securing Sex: Morality and repression in the making of cold war Brazil*. Chapel Hill: University of North Carolina Press.

Dress for Success. (2006). Mission. Retrieved from www.dressforsuccess.org.

Fessler, L. (2017). What's wrong with this picture: Pornhub, the web's biggest porn site, is now teaching sex ed. *Quartz*.

Frederick, W. C. (1998). Moving to CSR: What to pack for the trip. *Business and Society, 37*(1), 40–59. https://doi.org/10.1177/000765039803700103.

Gond, J., Igalens, J., Swaen, V., & Akremi, A. (2011). The human resources contribution to responsible leadership: An exploration of the CSR-HR interface. *Journal of Business Ethics, 98*, 115–132.

Itani, S. (2017). *The ideological evolution of human resource management: A critical look into HRM research and practices*. Bingley: Emerald.

Kalenda, J. (2016). Pornography as part of the socio-cultural changes in Kubátová. In H. Kubátová, K. Čada, M. Fafejta, I. Chorvát, K. Ivanová, E. Jarošová, J. Kalenda, L. Křeménková, D. Lužný, & E. Moravčíková (Eds.), *Ways of Life in the Late Modernity*. Czech Republic: Univerzita Palackého v Olomouci.

Klikauer, T. (2014). *Seven moralities of human resource management*. United Kingdom: Palgrave Macmillan.

Kopp, D. M. (2018). *Famous (and infamous) training: A social history of training and development*. New York: Palgrave Macmillan.

Kulik, C. T., Bainbridge, H. T. J., & Cregan, C. (2008). Known by the company we keep: Stigma-by-association effects in the workplace. *Academy of Management Review, 33*(1), 216–230.

Orenstein, P. (2017). *Girls & sex: Navigating the complicated new landscape*. New York: Harper Paperbacks.

Österberg, J. (2012). *Self and others: A study of ethical egoism*. Dordrecht: Springer Netherlands.

Smith, J. (2014). Charities won't take porn money unless they can keep it a dirty secret. *Observer*.

U.S. Department of Justice. (2000). *Al Queda training manual*. Washington, DC: Department of Justice.

Watts, P. (1999). *Corporate social responsibility: Meeting changing expectations*. Dorset: World Business Council for Sustainable Development.

Waytz, A., Epley, N., & Cacioppo, J. (2010). Social cognition unbound: Insights into anthropomorphism and dehumanization. *Current Directions in Psychological Science, 19*(1), 58–62.

Werner, J. M., & DeSimone, R. L. (2011). *Human resource development*. Mason: Cengage Learning.

Index

D. M. Kopp, *Human Resource Management in the Pornography Industry*, https://doi.org/10.1007/978-3-030-37659-8

The manufacturer's authorised representative in the EU is Springer Nature Customer Service Centre GmbH, Europaplatz 3, 69115 Heidelberg, Germany. If you have any concerns regarding our products, please contact ProductSafety@springernature.com

Printed and bound by CPI Group (UK) Ltd, Croydon, CR0 4YY

30/09/2026

02225475-0003